FOLK SONGS FOR BANJO

40 TRADITIONAL AMERICAN FOLK SONGS
ARRANGED FOR CLAWHAMMER BANJO

ARRANGED BY  MICHAEL MILES

ISBN 978-1-61780-417-5

7777 W. BLUEMOUND RD. P.O. BOX 13819 MILWAUKEE, WI 53213

In Australia Contact:
Hal Leonard Australia Pty. Ltd.
4 Lentara Court
Cheltenham, Victoria, 3192 Australia
Email: ausadmin@halleonard.com.au

Visit Hal Leonard Online at
www.halleonard.com

T0057800

CONTENTS

Amazing Grace

Words by John Newton
Traditional American Melody

G tuning:
(5th-1st) G-D-G-B-D

Key of G

Verse
Moderately

1. A - maz - ing grace how sweet the

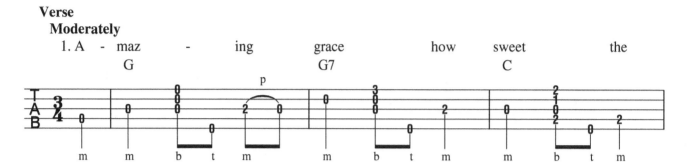

sound that saved a wretch like

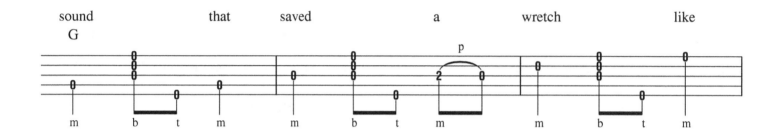

me. I once was

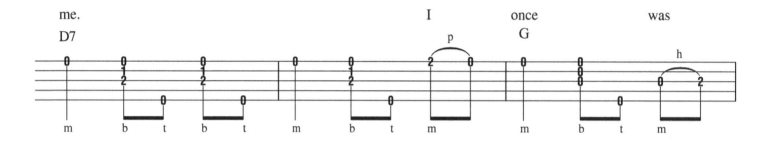

lost but now I'm found, was

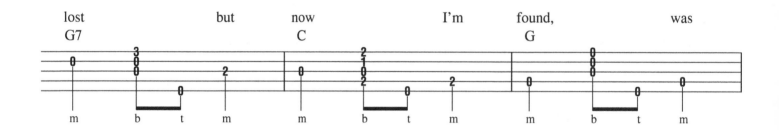

blind but now I see.

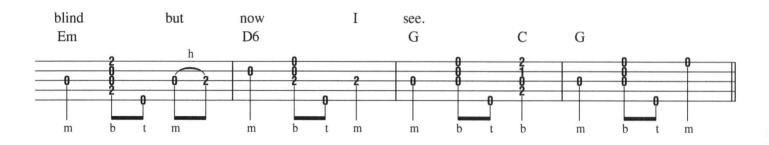

Banjo Break

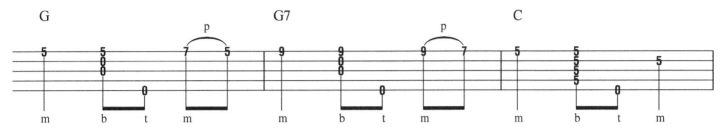

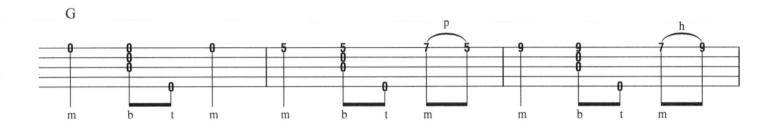

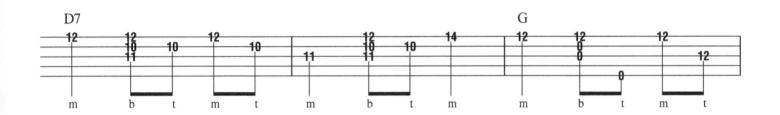

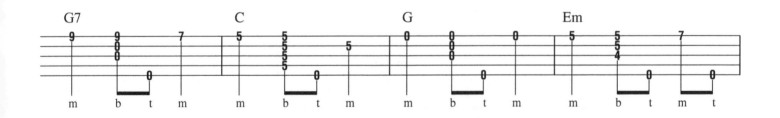

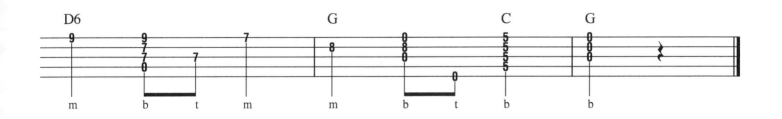

Arkansas Traveler

Southern American Folksong

Double C tuning, capo II:
(5th-1st) G-C-G-C-D

Key of D

*Left hand pull-off to adjacent string.

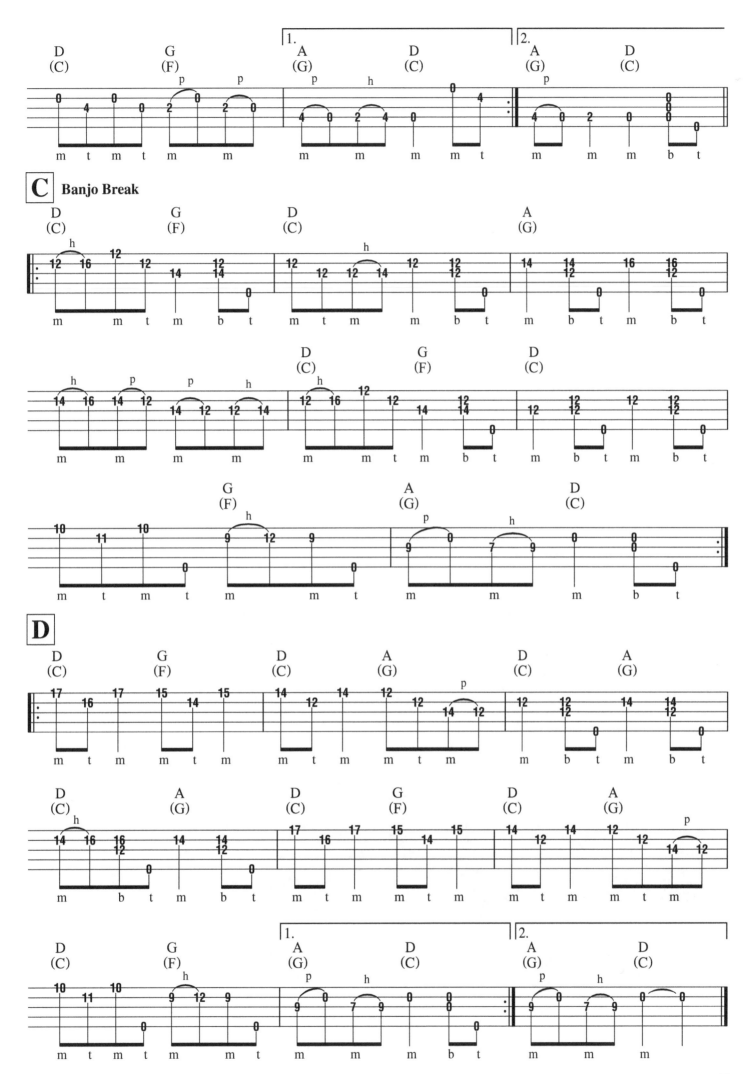

C Banjo Break

D

Beautiful Brown Eyes

Traditional

G tuning:
(5th-1st) G-D-G-B-D

Key of G

Verse
Moderately slow

1. Wil - lie, oh, Wil - lie, I love you,

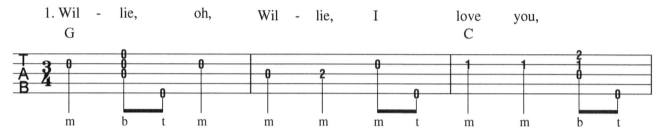

I love you with all of my

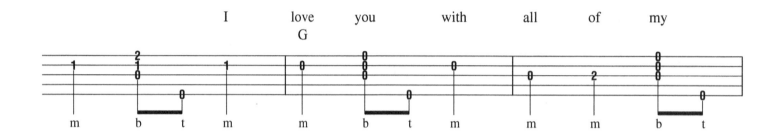

heart. To - mor - row we

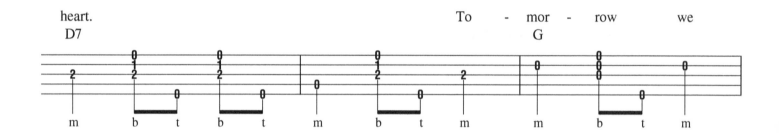

might have been mar - ried, but

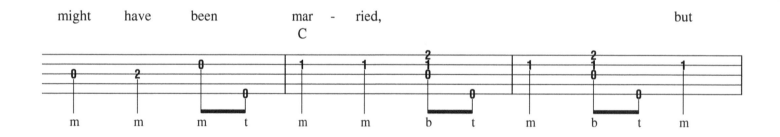

drink - ing has kept us a - part.

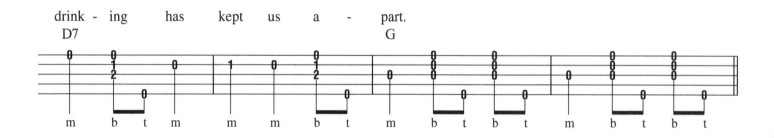

Chorus

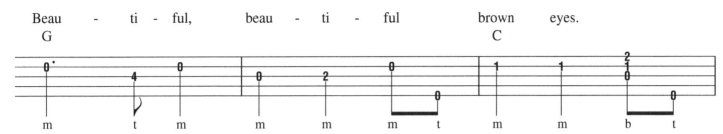

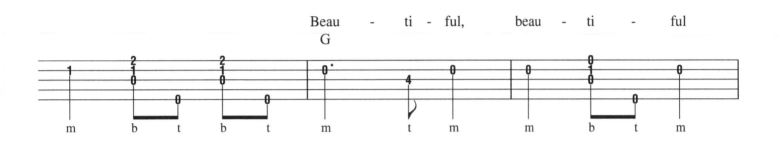

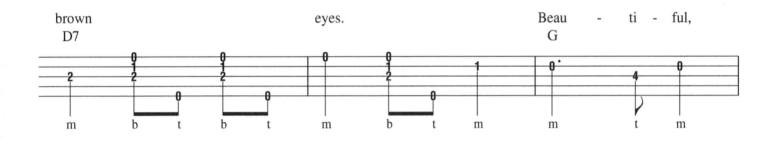

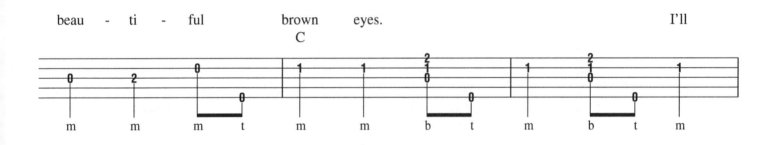

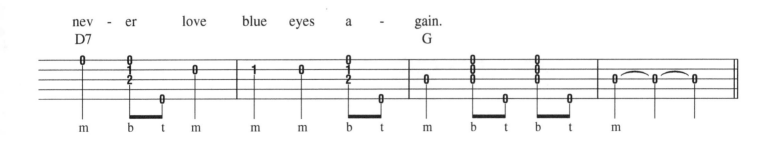

Banjo Break

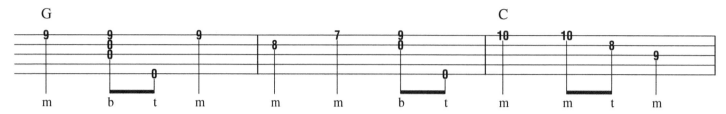

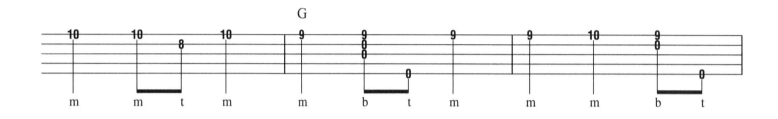

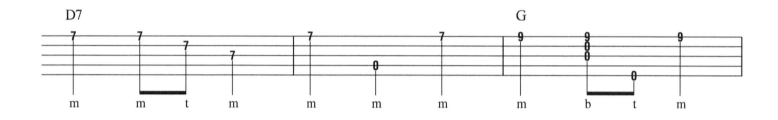

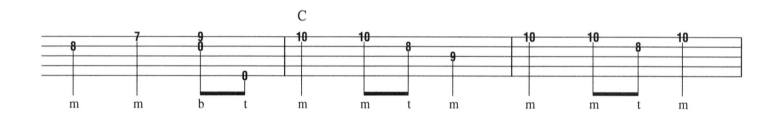

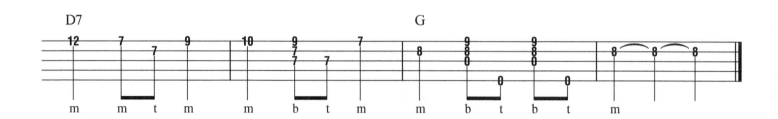

(I Wish I Was In) Dixie

Words and Music by Daniel Decatur Emmett

Double C tuning:
(5th-1st) G-C-G-C-D

Key of C

Verse
Moderately

1. Oh, I wish I was in the land of cot - ton. Old times there were

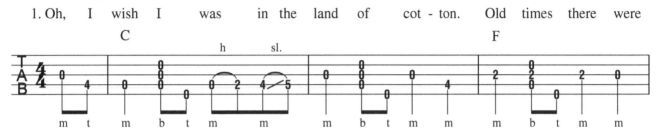

not for - got - ten. Look a - way, look a - way, look a -

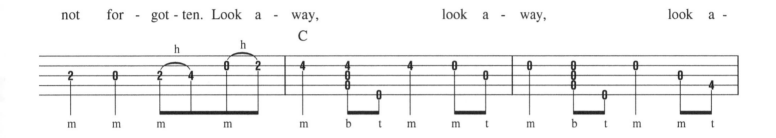

way, Dix - ie - land. In Dix - ie - land, where

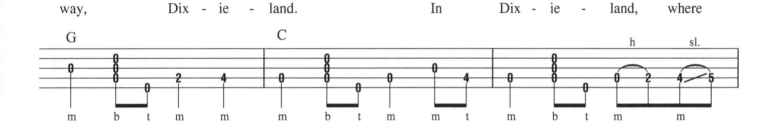

I was born, ear - ly on one frost - y morn- in'. Look a -

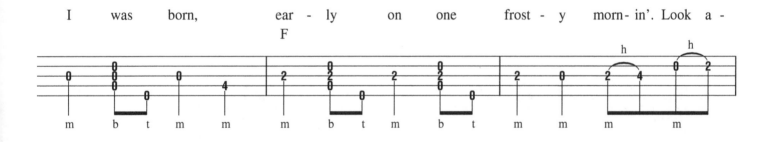

way, look a - way, look a - way, Dix - ie - land. Well, I

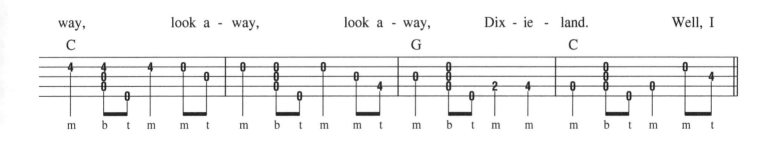

Chorus

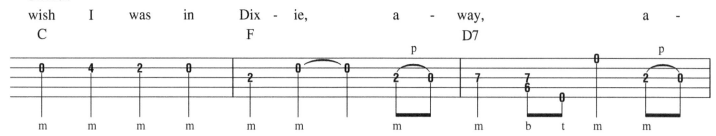

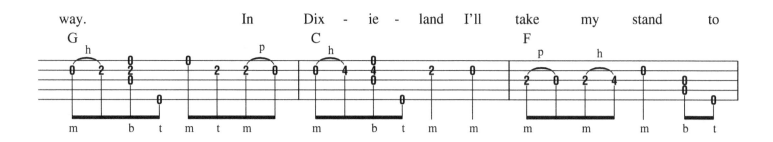

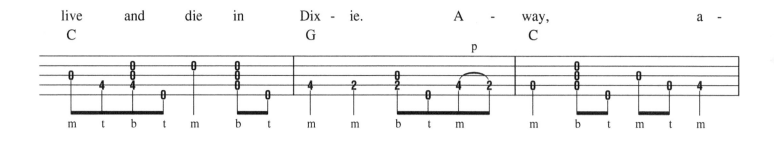

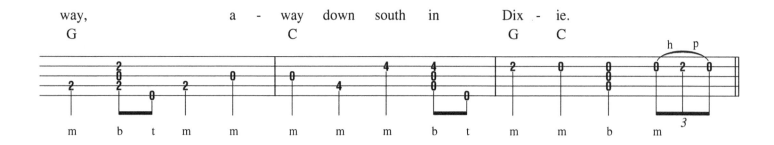

Banjo Break

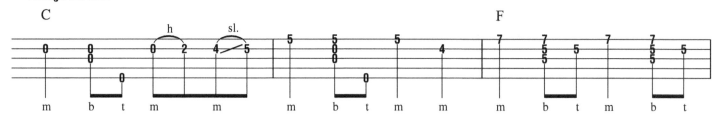

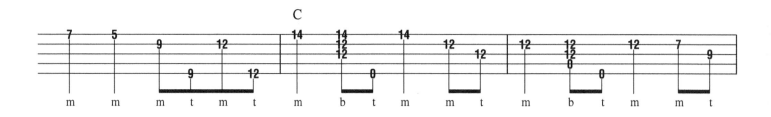

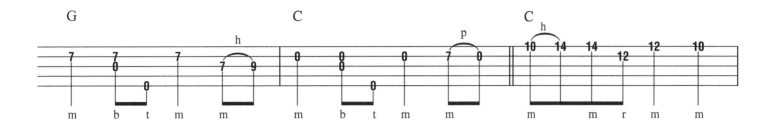

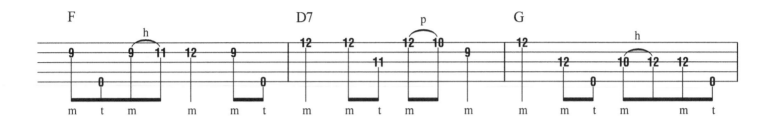

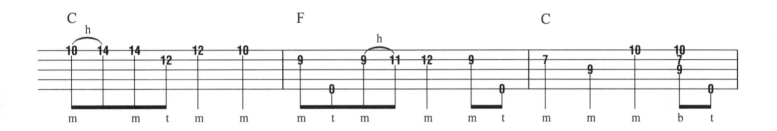

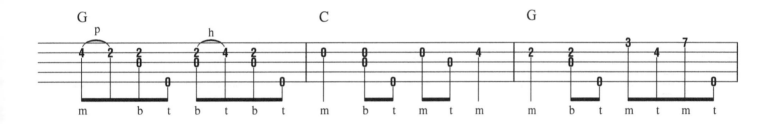

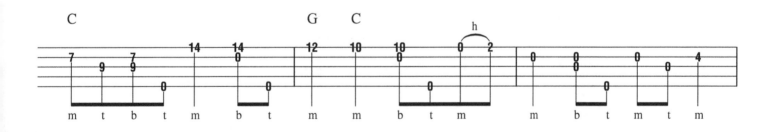

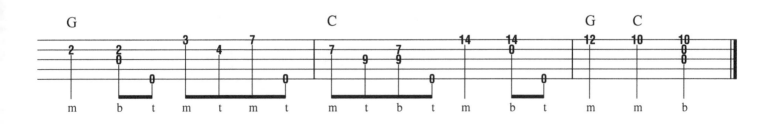

The Blue Tail Fly
(Jimmy Crack Corn)

Words and Music by Daniel Decatur Emmett

G tuning:
(5th-1st) G-D-G-B-D

Key of G

Verse
Moderately fast

1. When I was young I used to wait on mas - ter, hand - ing

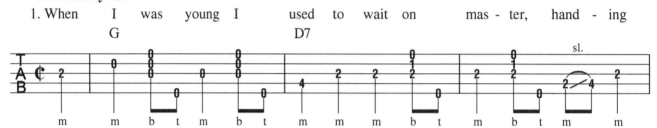

him his plate. I brought his bot - tle when he was dry and

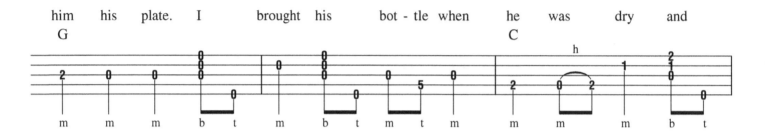

brushed a - way the blue - tail fly. **Chorus** Jim - my crack corn and

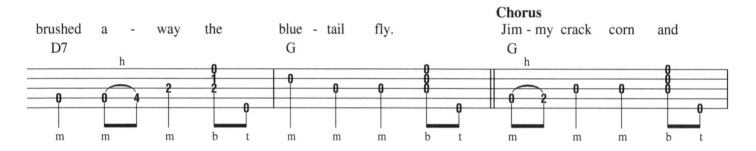

I don't care, Jim - my crack corn and I don't care,

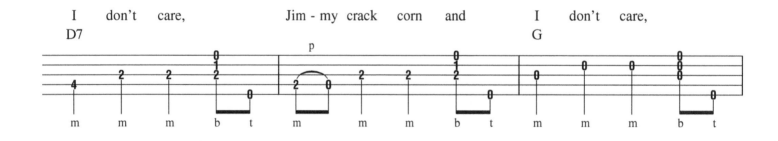

Jim - my crack corn and I don't care, old mas - ter's gone a - way.

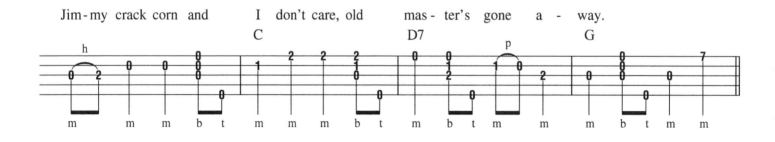

Banjo Break

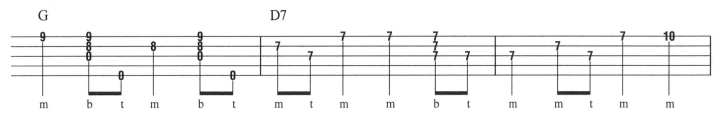

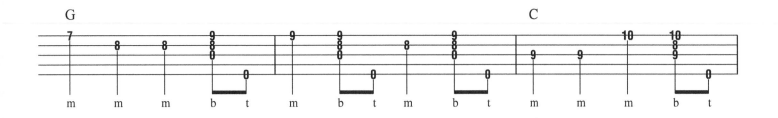

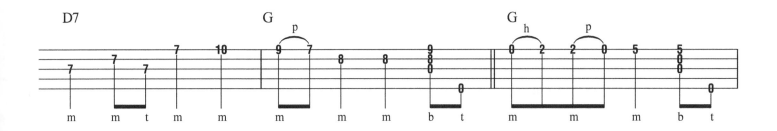

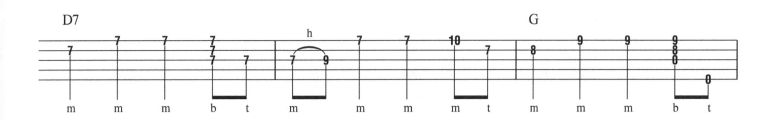

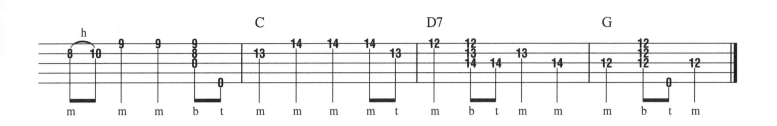

Buffalo Gals
(Won't You Come Out Tonight?)

Words and Music by Cool White (John Hodges)

G tuning:
(5th-1st) G-D-G-B-D

Key of G

Verse
Moderately

1. As I was walk-ing down the street, down the street,

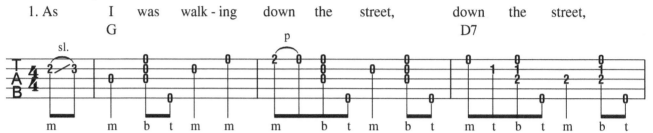

down the street, a pretty lit-tle girl I chanced to meet and we

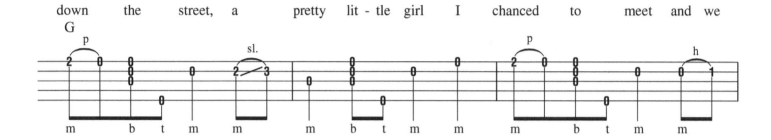

danced by the light of the moon. **Chorus** Buf-fa-lo gals, won't you

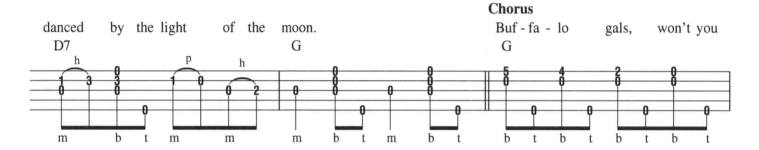

come out to-night, come out to-night, come out to-night?

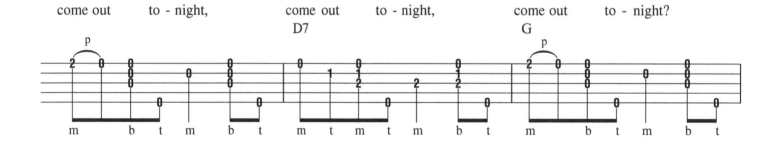

Buf-fa-lo gals, won't you come out to-night and

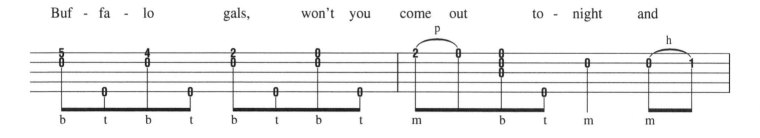

dance   by   the light   of   the moon?

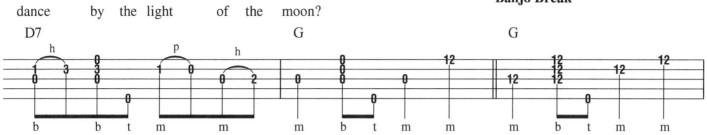

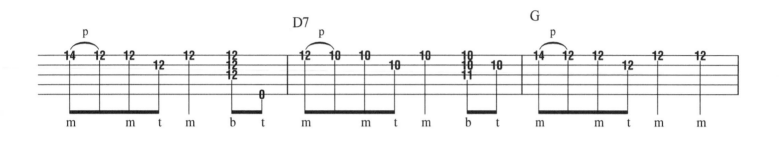

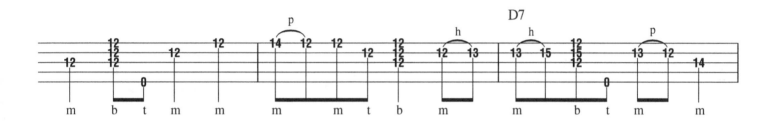

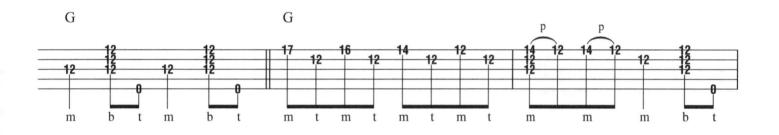

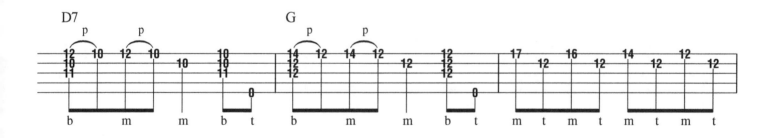

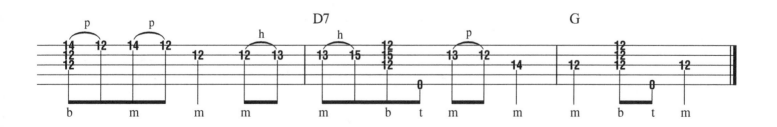

Carry Me Back to Old Virginny

Words and Music by James A. Bland

G tuning:
(5th-1st) G-D-G-B-D

Key of G

Verse
Moderately fast

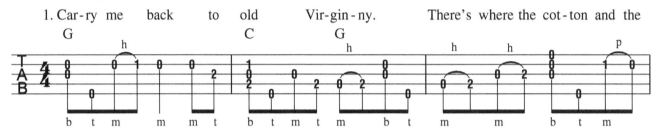

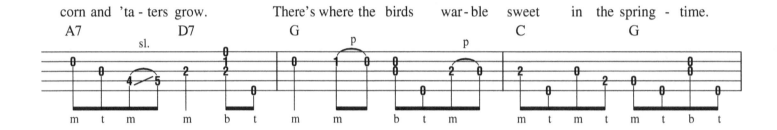

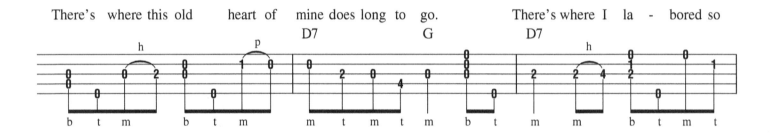

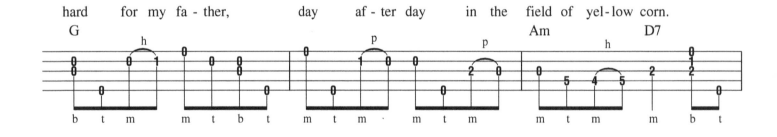

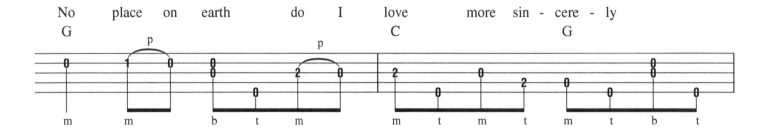

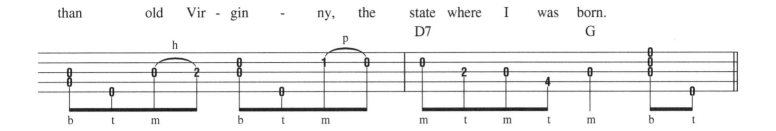

than old Vir - gin - ny, the state where I was born.

Banjo Break

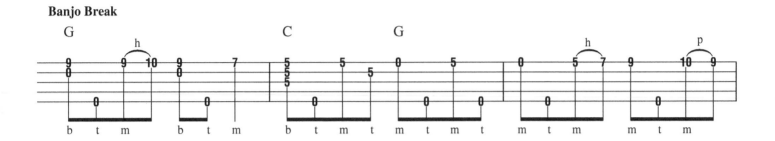

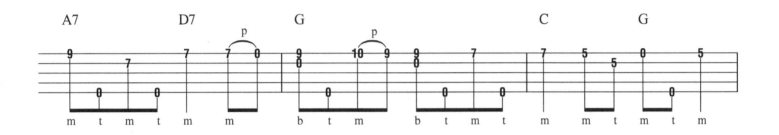

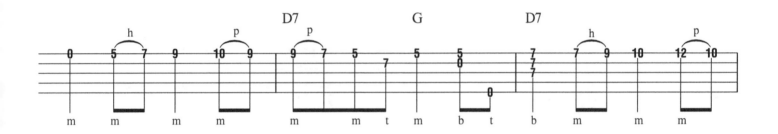

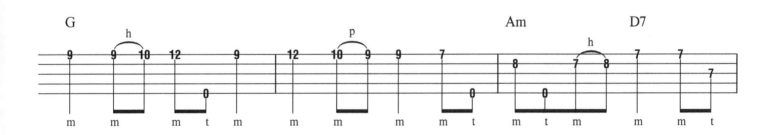

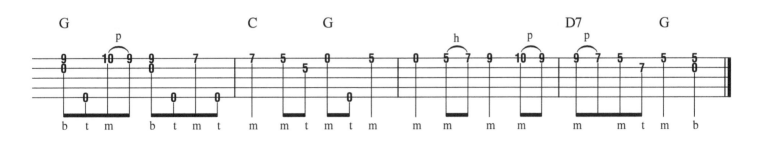

Comin' Through the Rye

By Robert Burns

G tuning:
(5th-1st) G-D-G-B-D

Key of G

Verse
Slowly

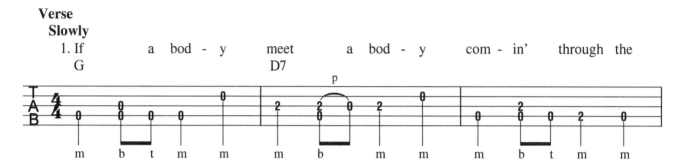

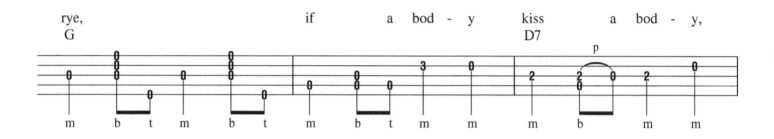

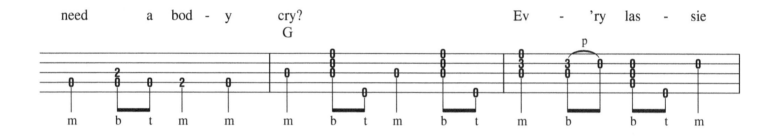

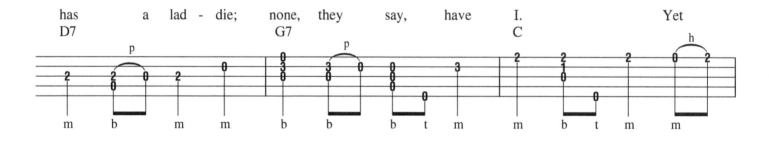

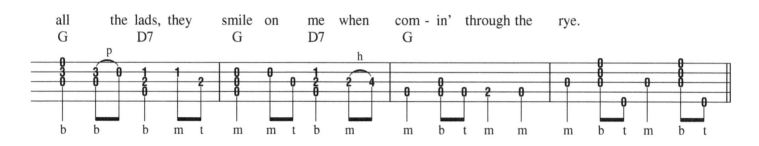

Banjo Break

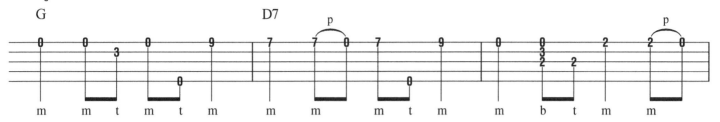

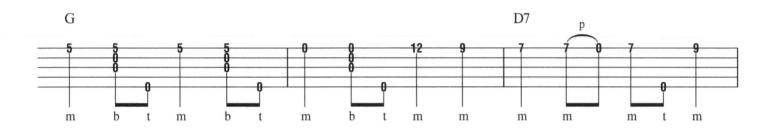

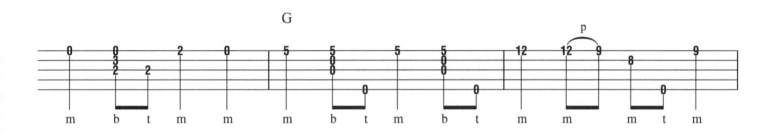

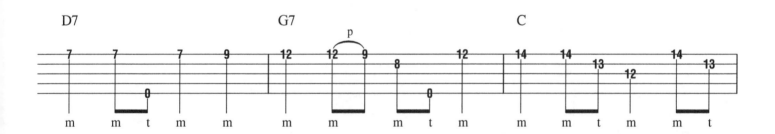

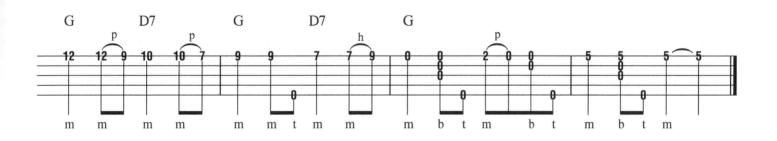

The Crawdad Song

Traditional

G tuning:
(5th-1st) G-D-G-B-D

Key of G

Verse
Moderately fast

You get a line and I'll get a pole, hon - ey.

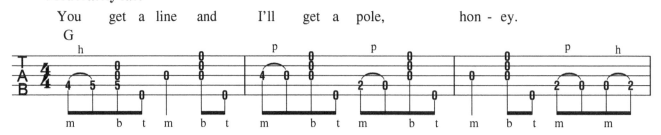

You get a line and I'll get a pole,

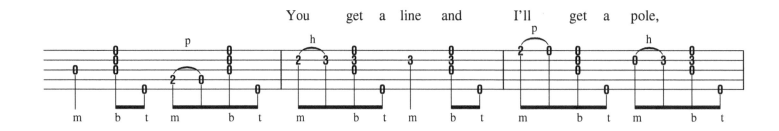

babe. You get a line and

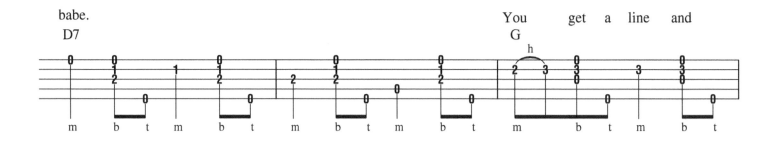

I'll get a pole. We'll go down to the craw - dad hole.

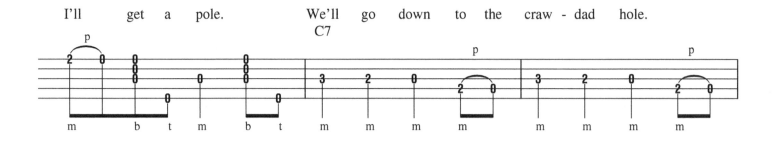

Hon- ey, ba - by, mine.

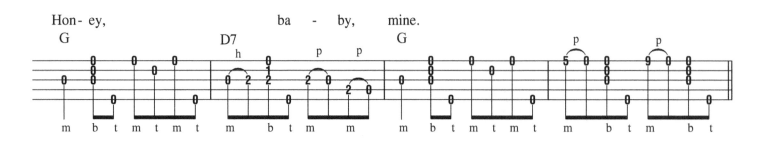

Banjo Break

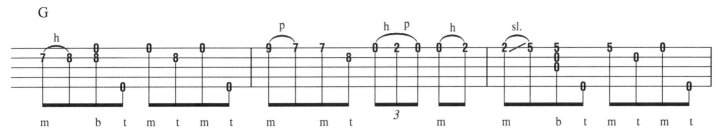

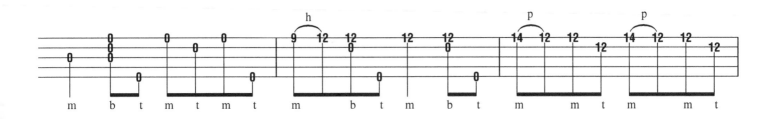

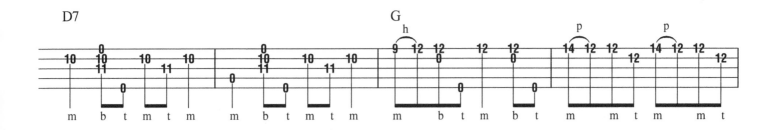

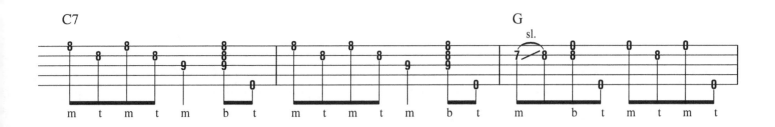

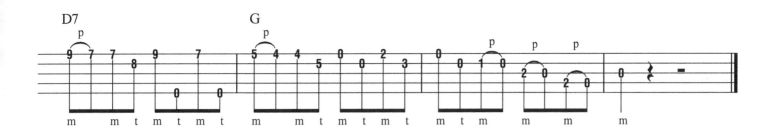

Down by the Riverside

African American Spiritual

G tuning:
(5th-1st) G-D-G-B-D

Key of G

Verse
Moderately

1. Gon-na   lay   down   my   bur - den   down   by   the

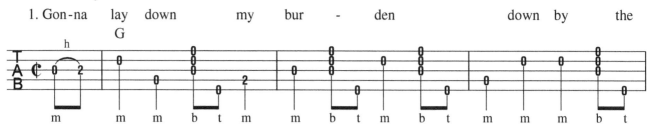

riv - er - side,   down   by   the   riv - er - side,

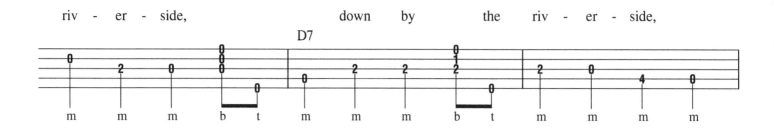

down   by   the   riv - er - side.   Gon - na   lay   down   my

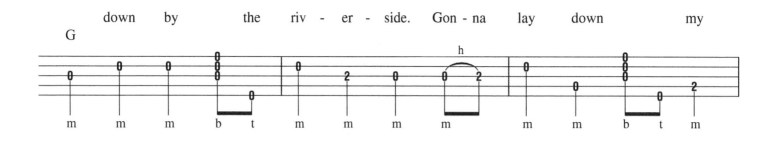

bur - den   down   by   the   riv - er - side   and

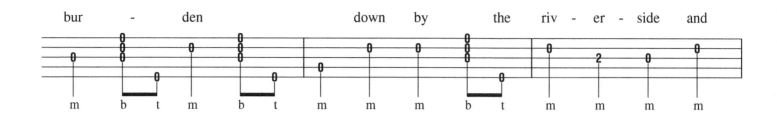

stud - y   war   no   more.   I   ain't   gonna

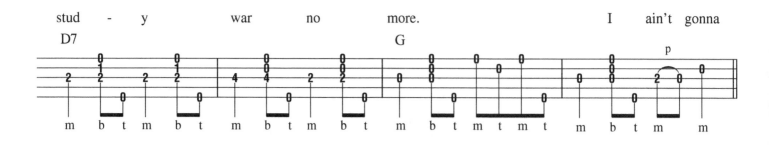

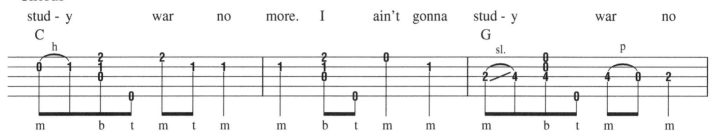

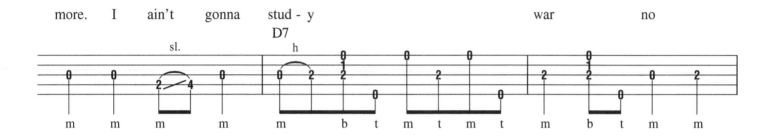

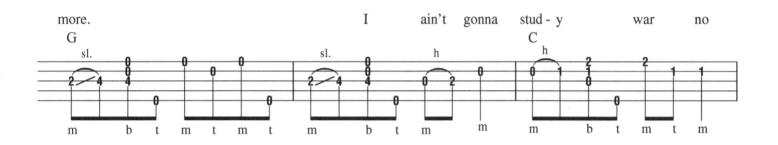

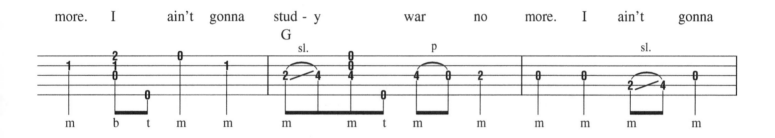

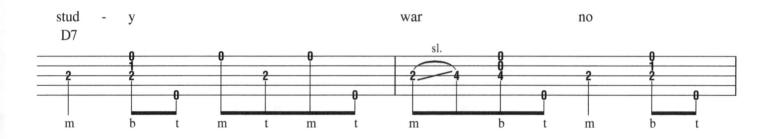

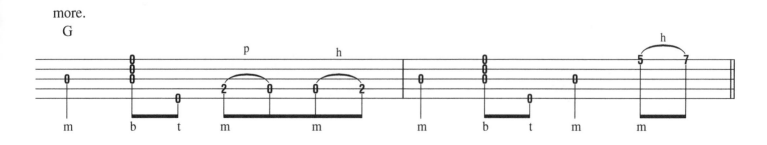

Banjo Break

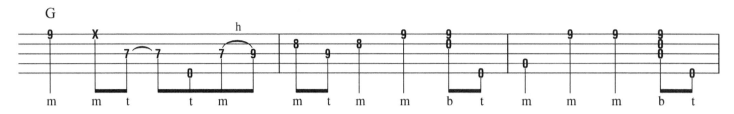

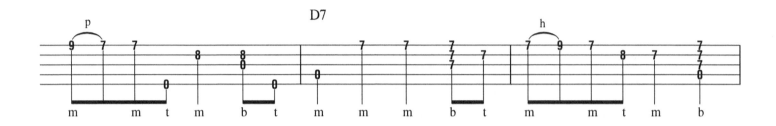

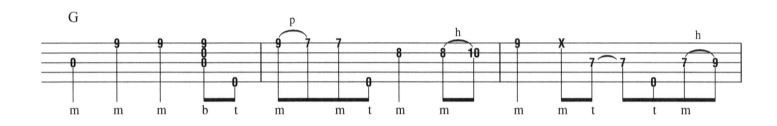

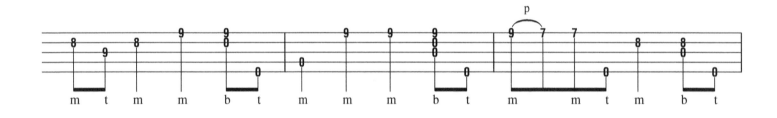

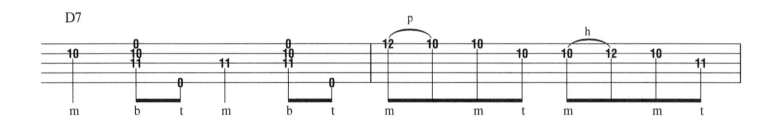

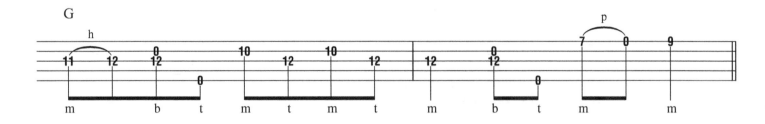

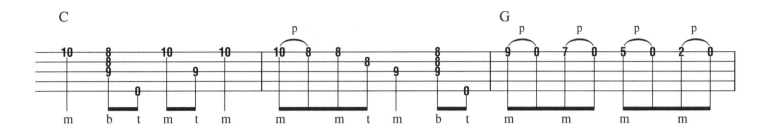

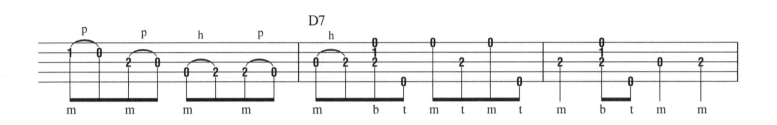

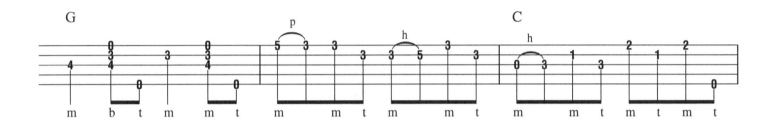

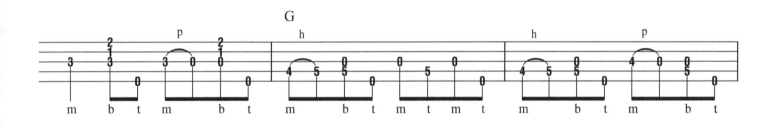

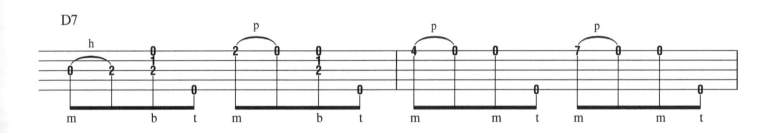

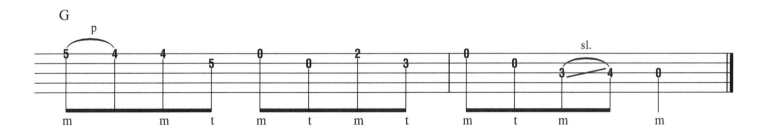

Down in the Valley

Traditional American Folksong

G tuning:
(5th-1st) G-D-G-B-D

Key of G

Verse
Moderately slow

1. Down   in   the   val   -   ley,

G

val - ley   so   low,

D7

late   in   the   eve   -   ning

hear   the   train   blow.

G

Hear   that   train   blow   -   ing,   hear   that   train blow.   Hang   your   head

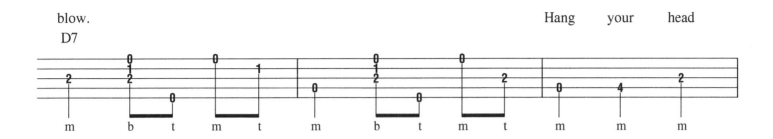

o   -   ver,   hear   that   train

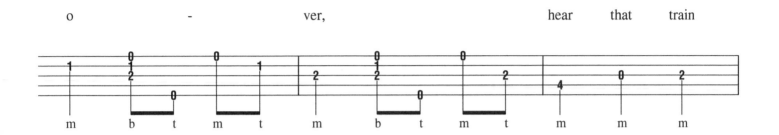

blow.   **Banjo Break**

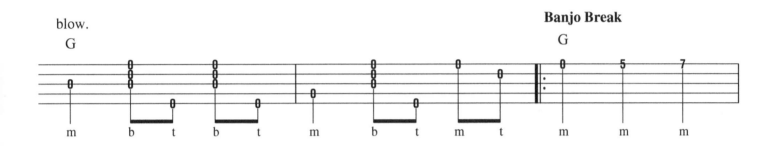

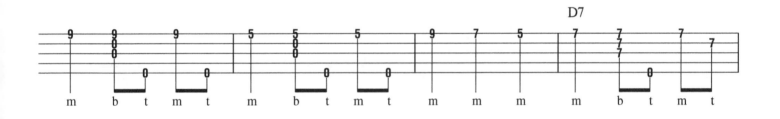

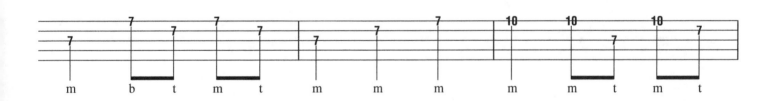

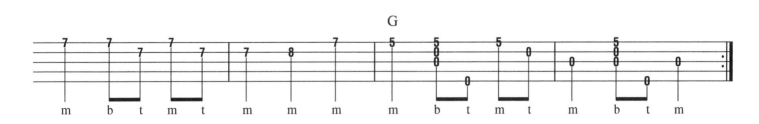

Freight Train

Words and Music by Elizabeth Cotten

C tuning:
(5th-1st) G-C-G-C-E

Key of C

Verse
Fast

1. Freight train, freight train, run so

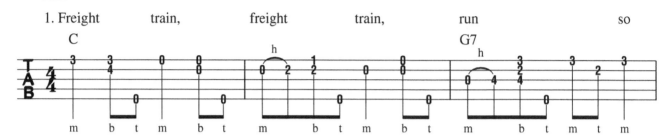

fast. Freight train, freight train,

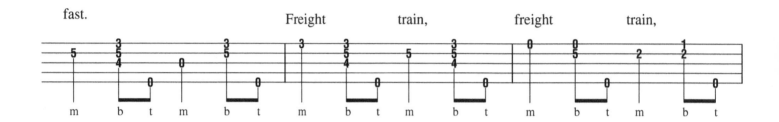

run so fast. Please don't

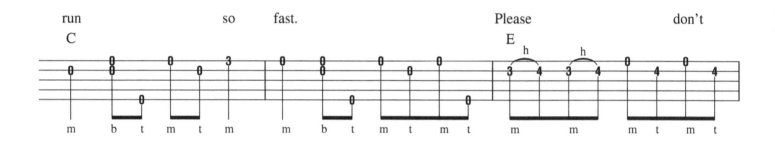

tell what train I'm on and they

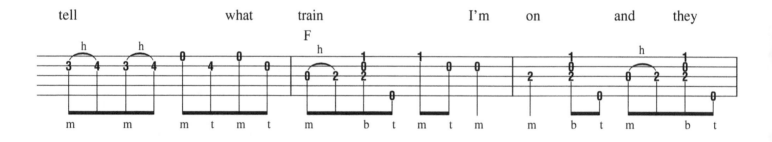

won't know where I've gone.

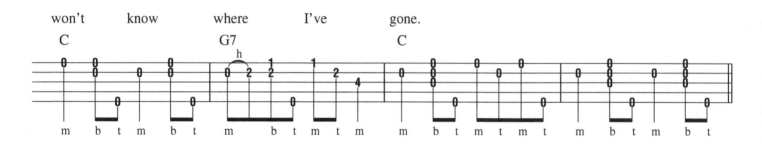

Banjo Break

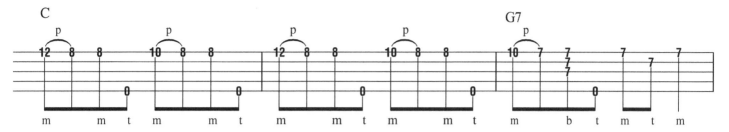

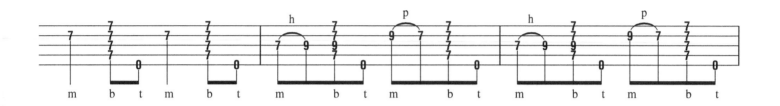

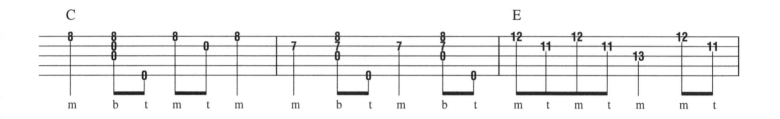

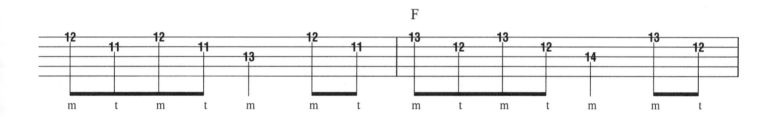

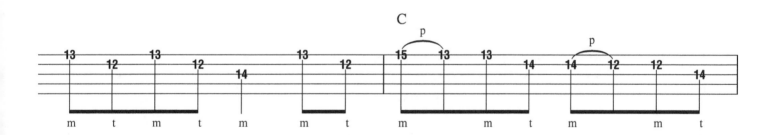

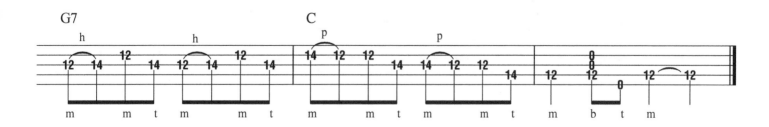

Give Me That Old Time Religion

Traditional

Double C tuning:
(5th-1st) G-C-G-C-D

Key of C

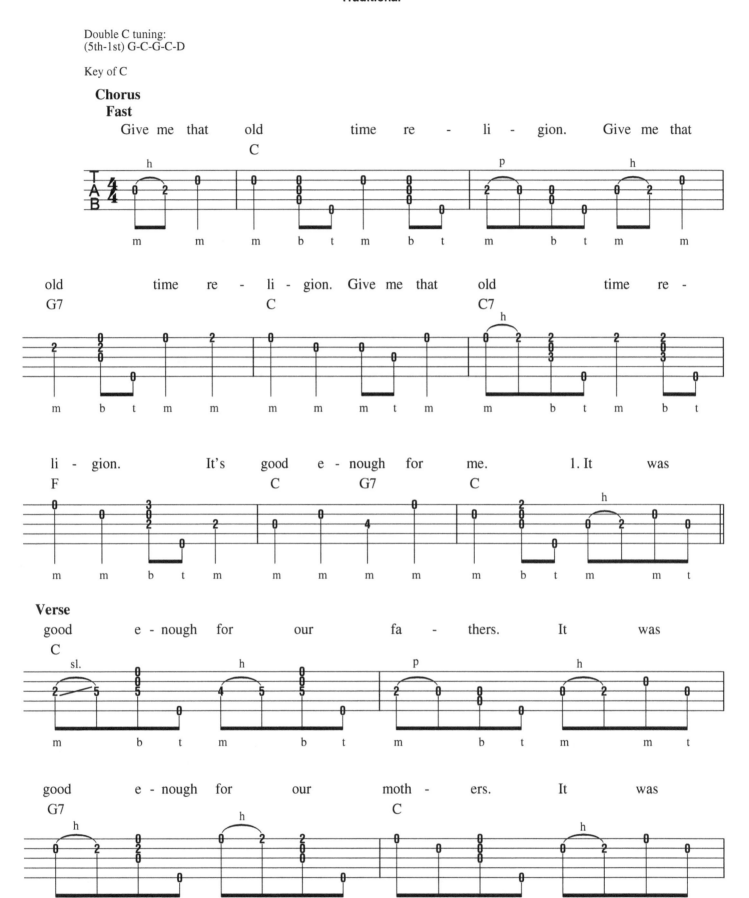

good   e - nough for   our   broth - ers.   So   it's

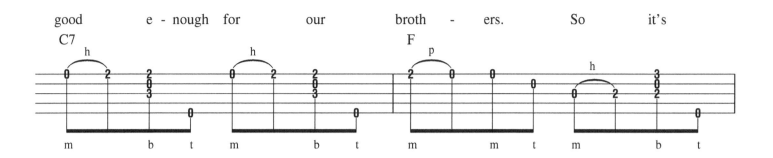

good   e -   nough   for   me.

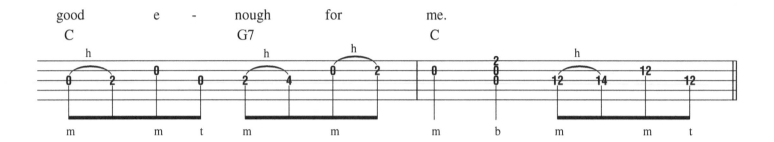

Banjo Break

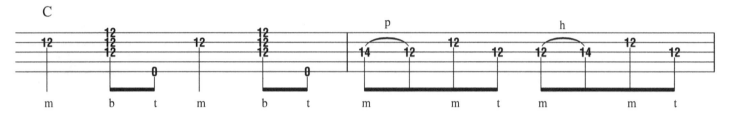

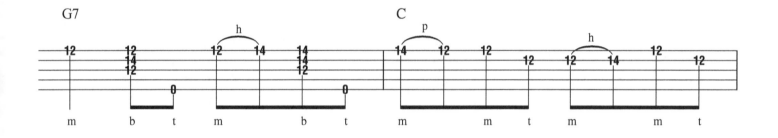

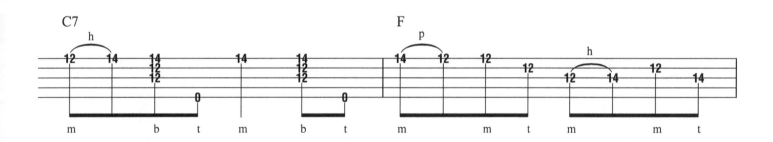

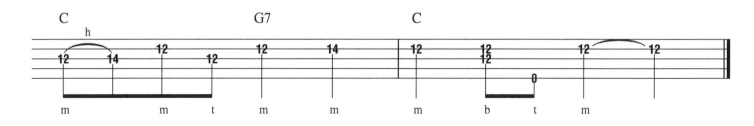

Good Night Ladies

Words by E.P. Christy
Traditional Music

G tuning:
(5th-1st) G-D-G-B-D

Key of G

Verse
Moderately fast

1. Good night, la - dies. Good night,

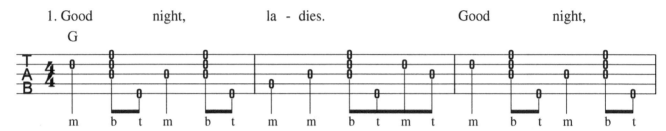

la - dies. Good night, la - dies. We're

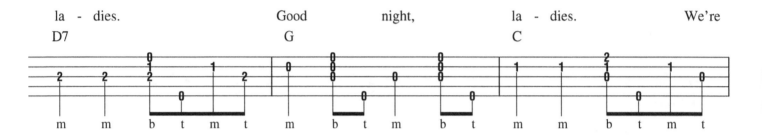

go - ing to leave you now. **Chorus** Mer - ri - ly we

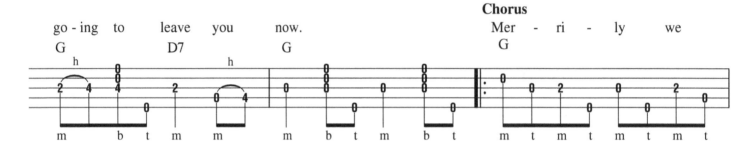

roll a - long, roll a - long,

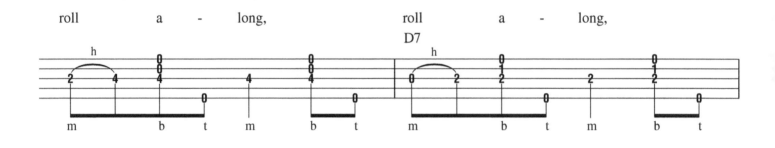

roll a - long. Mer - ri - ly we

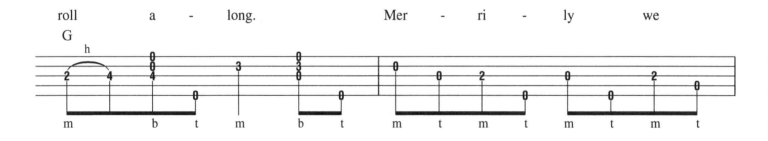

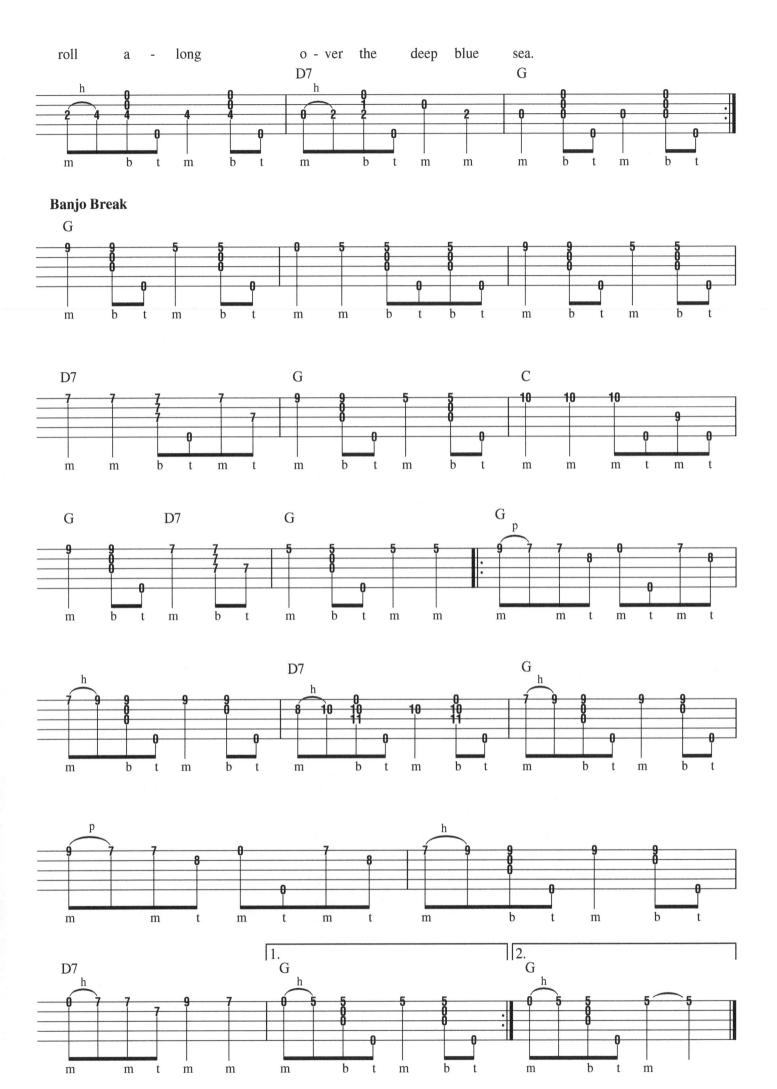

Banjo Break

Hail, Hail, the Gang's All Here

Words by D.A. Esrom
Music by Theodore F. Morse and Arthur Sullivan

G tuning:
(5th-1st) G-D-G-B-D

Key of G

Verse
Moderately fast

1. Hail   hail,   the gang's all   here.   What the heck do we   care,

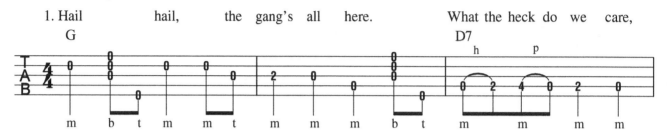

what the heck do we   care?   Hail   hail,   the gang's all   here.

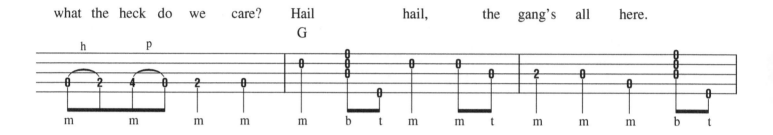

What the heck do we   care   now!   **Banjo Break**

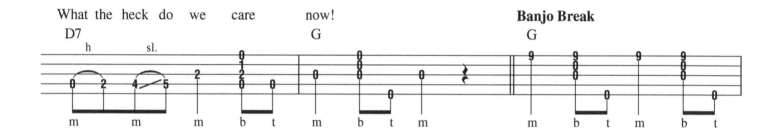

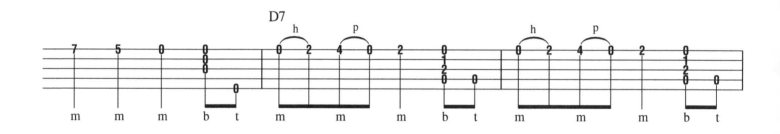

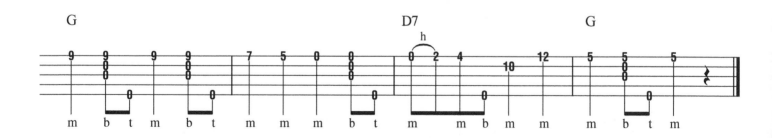

Home on the Range

Lyrics by Dr. Brewster Higley
Music by Dan Kelly

Double C tuning:
(5th-1st) G-C-G-C-D

Key of C

Verse
Moderately

1. Oh, give me a home where the buf - fa - lo

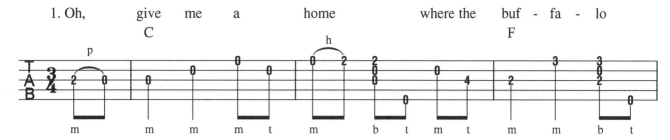

roam, where the deer and the an - te - lope play.

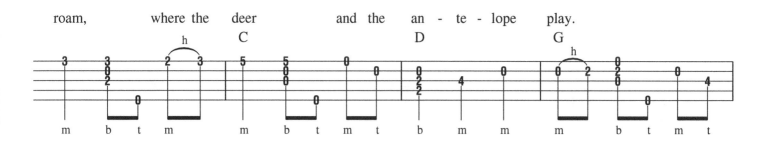

Where sel - dom is heard a dis - cour - ag - ing

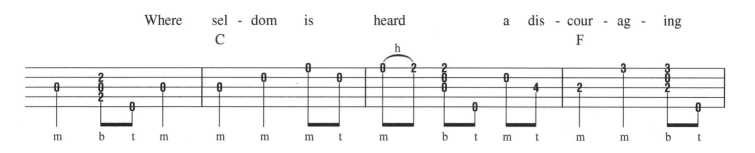

word, and the skies are not cloud - y all day.

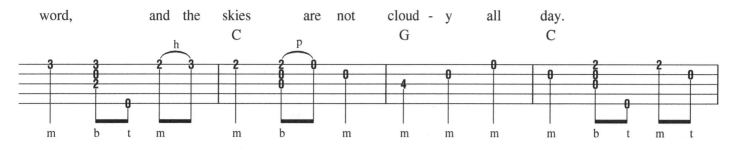

Chorus
Home, home on the range,

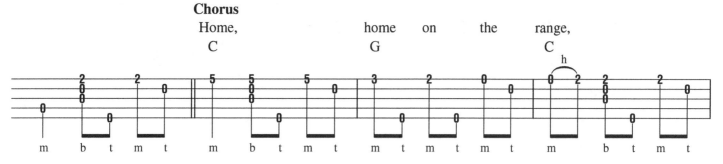

where the deer   and the   an - te - lope   play.

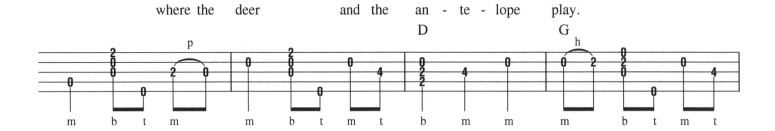

Where   sel - dom   is   heard   a   dis - cour - ag - ing

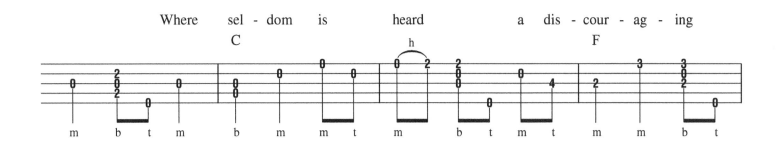

word,   and the   skies   are   not   cloud - y   all   day.

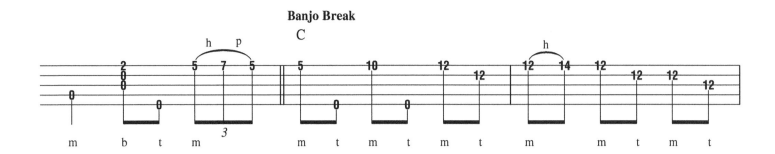

Banjo Break

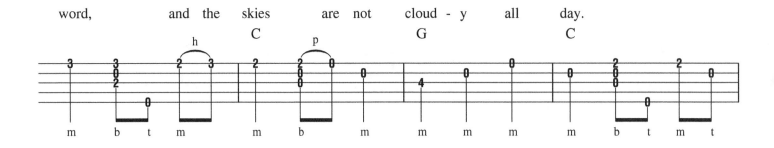

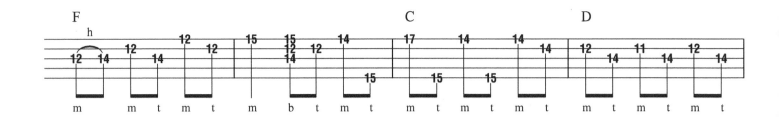

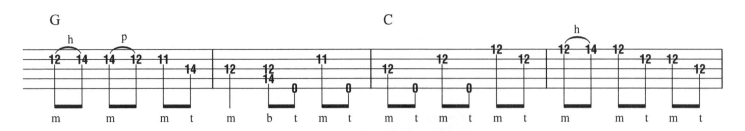

38

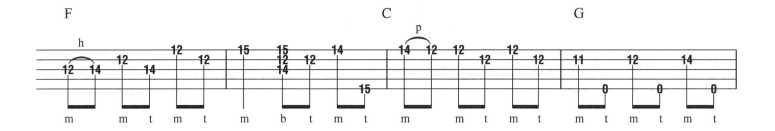

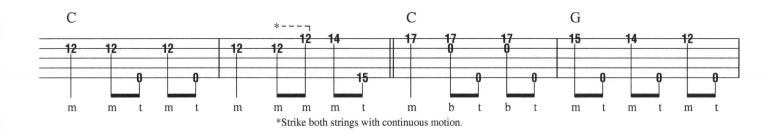

*Strike both strings with continuous motion.

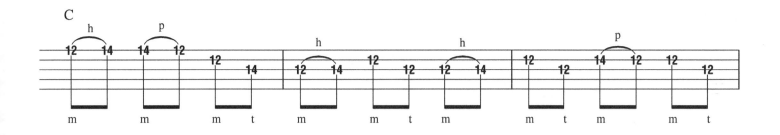

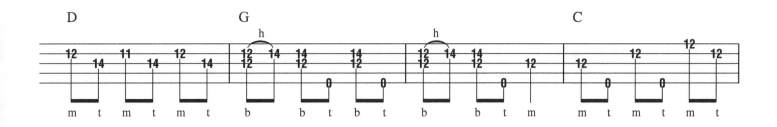

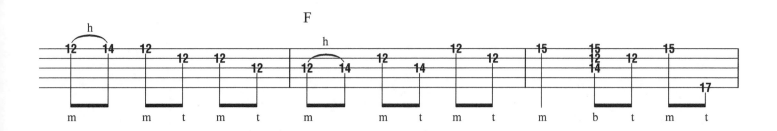

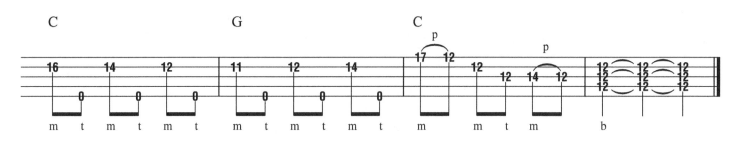

Home Sweet Home

Words by John Howard Payne
Music by Henry R. Bishop

G tuning:
(5th-1st) G-D-G-B-D

Key of G

Verse
Moderately

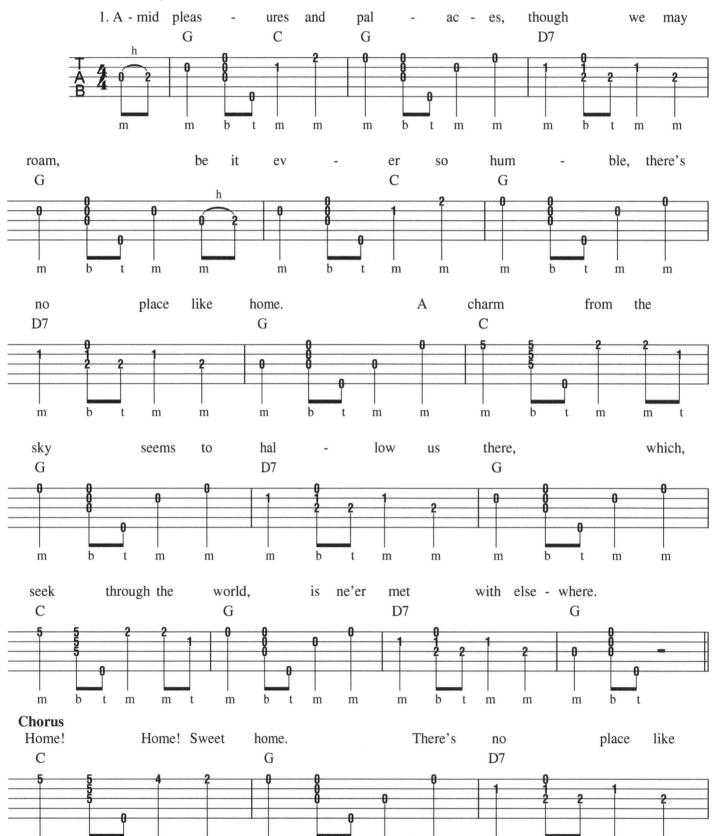

Chorus

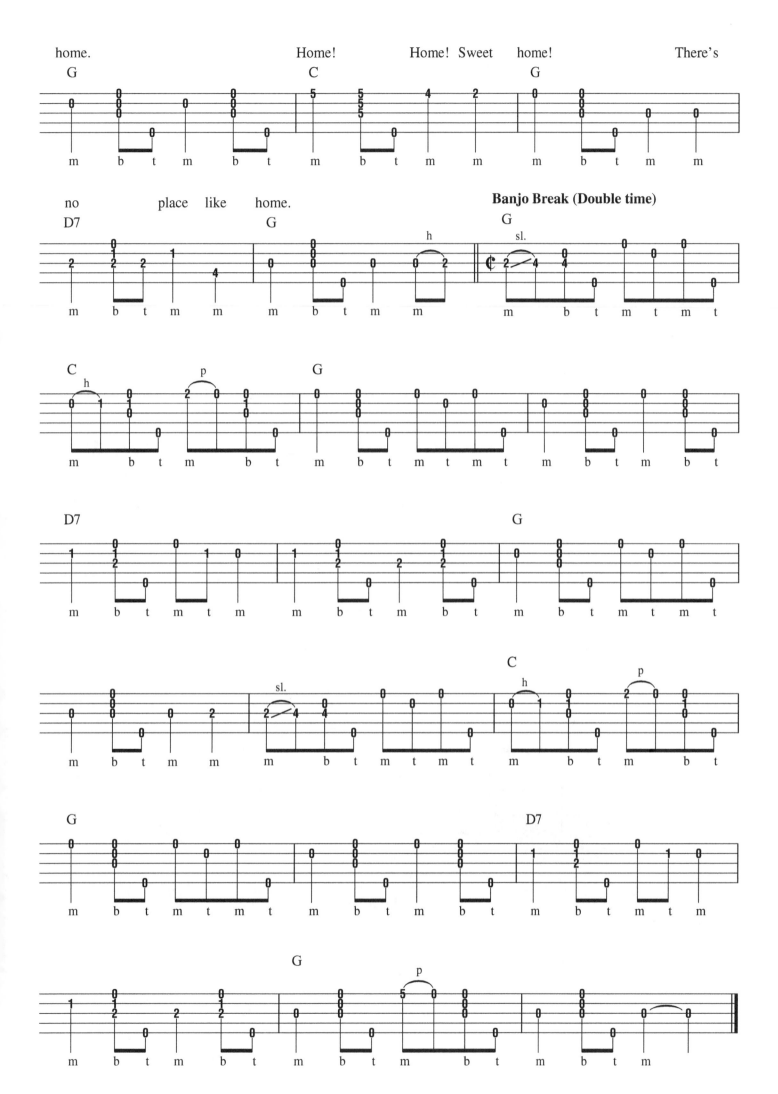

Banjo Break (Double time)

I've Been Working on the Railroad

American Folksong

C tuning:
(5th-1st) G-C-G-C-E

Key of C

Verse
Fast

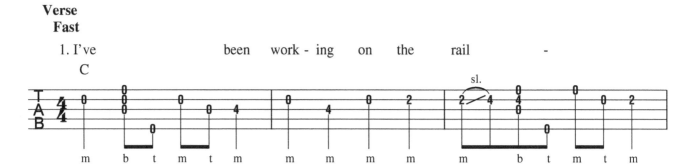

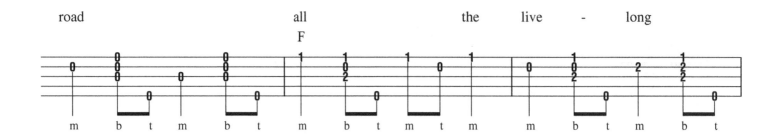

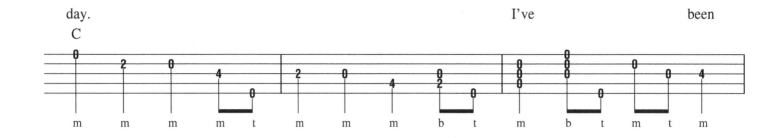

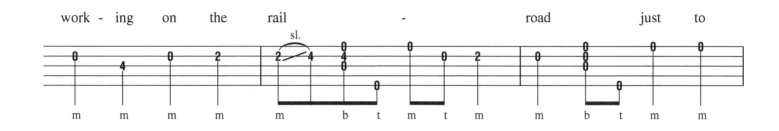

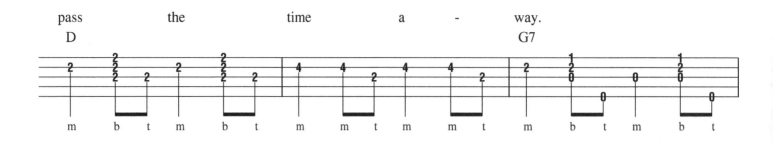

Can't you hear the whis - tle

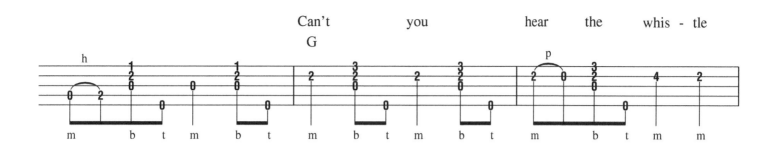

blow - ing? Rise up so

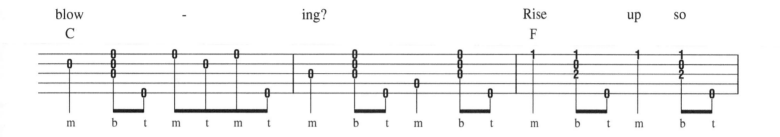

ear - ly in the morn.

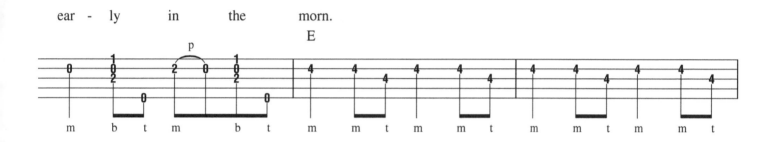

Can't you hear the cap - tain shout -

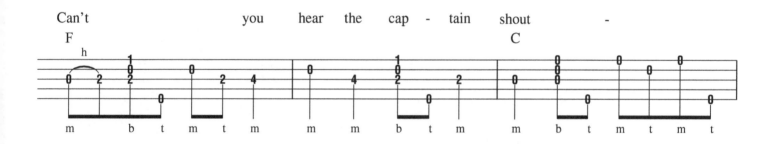

ing, "Di - nah, blow your

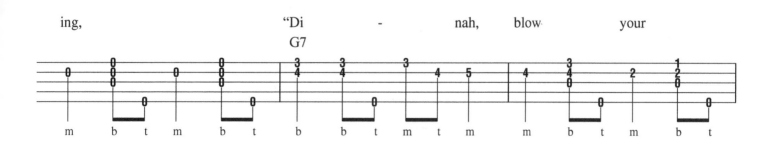

horn!"

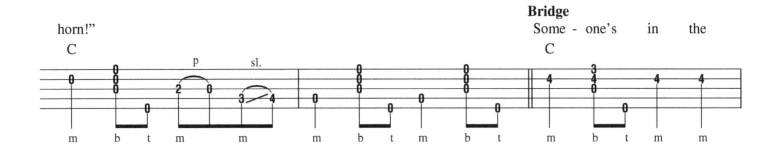

kitch - en with Di - nah.

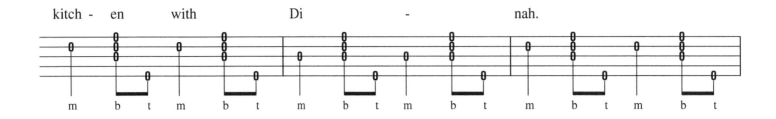

Some - one's in the kitch - en, I know.

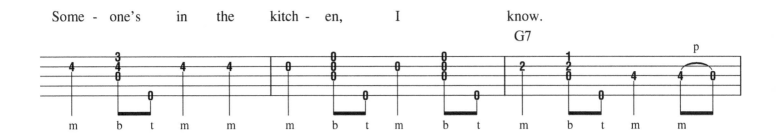

Some - one's in the kitch - en with

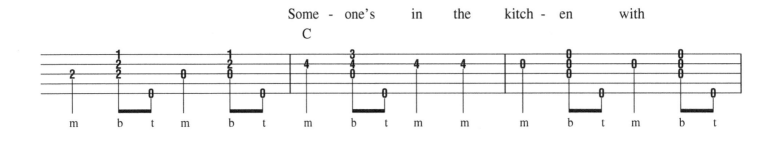

Di - nah, strum - min' on the

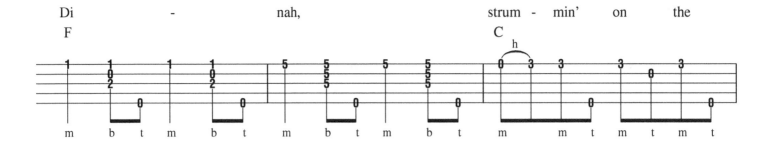

old ban - jo, and sing - in',

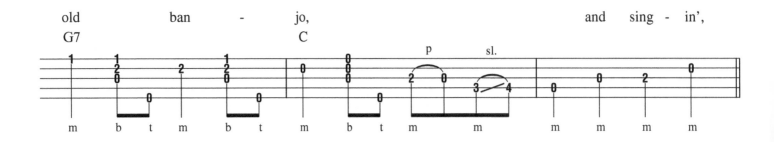

Chorus

"Fee,   fi,   fiddle - ee - i -

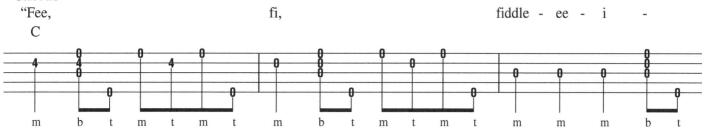

o,   fee,   fi,   fiddle - ee - i -

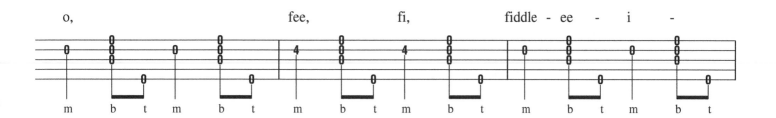

o,   fee,

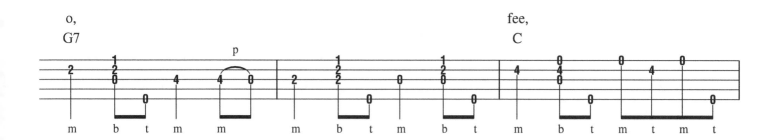

fi,   fiddle - ee - i - o."

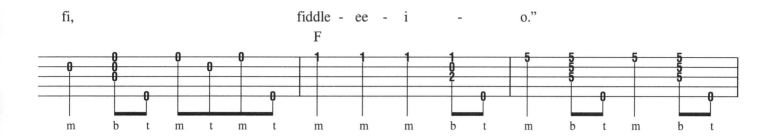

Strum - min'   on   the   old   ban -

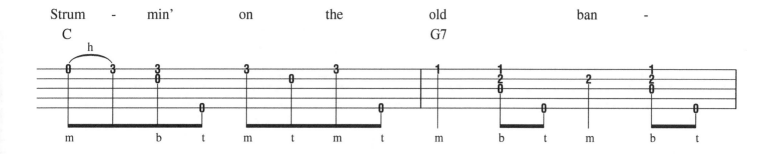

jo.

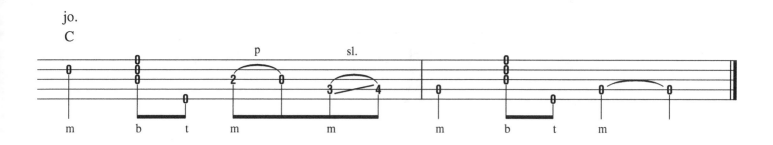

In the Good Old Summertime

Words by Ren Shields
Music by George Evans

G tuning:
(5th-1st) G-D-G-B-D

Key of G

Verse
Moderately

1. In the good old sum - mer - time,

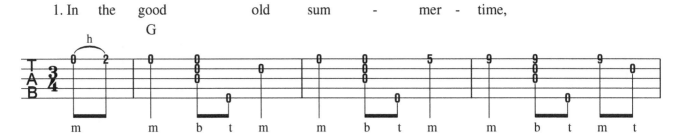

in the good old sum - mer -

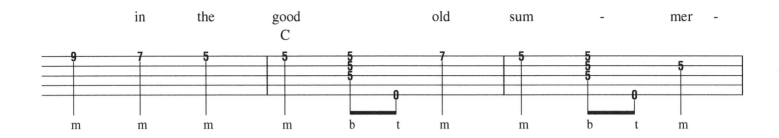

time, stroll - ing

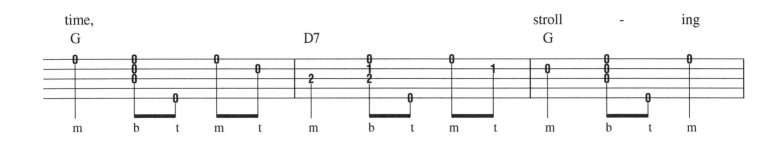

through the shad - y lanes

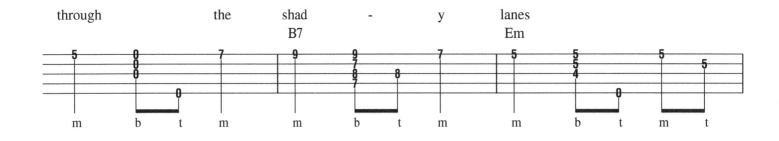

with your ba - by mine.

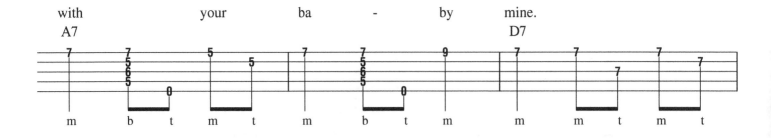

You hold her hand and

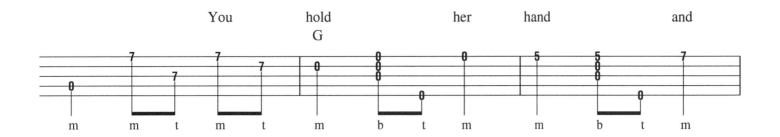

she holds yours and that's a

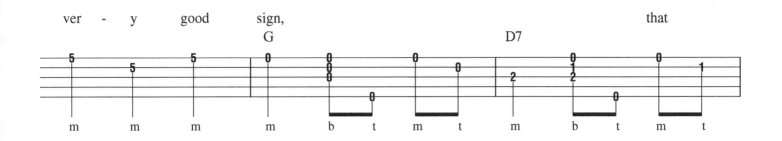

ver - y good sign, that

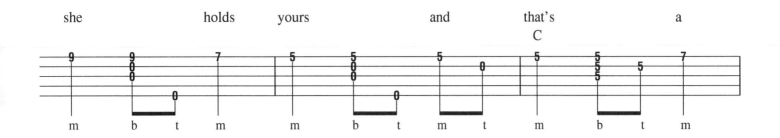

she's your toot - sie woot - sie in the

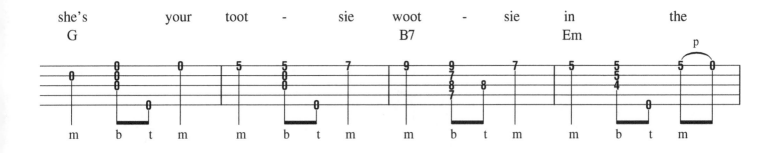

good old sum - mer - time.

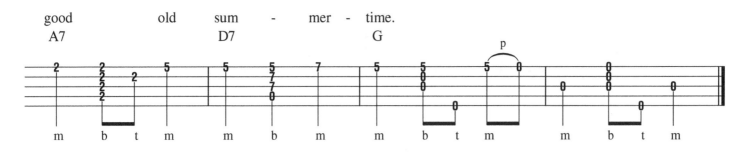

John Brown's Body

Traditional

G tuning:
(5th-1st) G-D-G-B-D

Key of G

Verse
Moderately fast

*Left hand pull-off to adjacent string.

Chorus

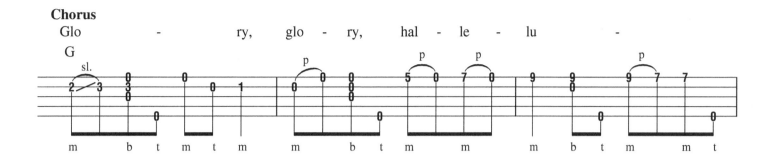

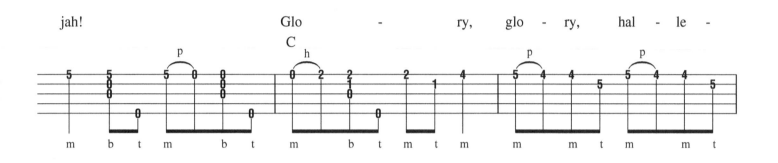

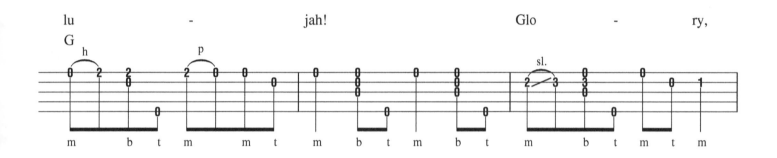

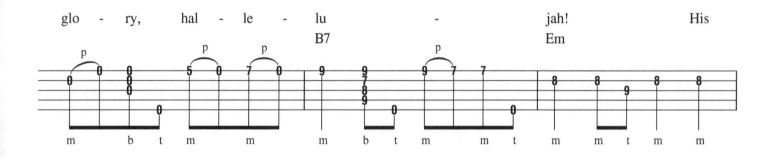

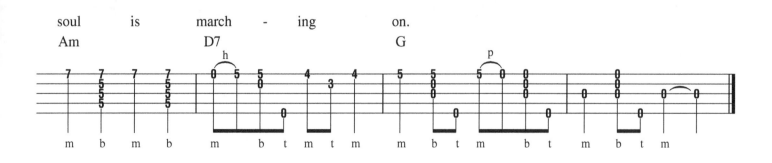

John Henry

West Virginia Folksong

Double C tuning:
(5th-1st) G-C-G-C-D

Key of C

Verse
Moderately

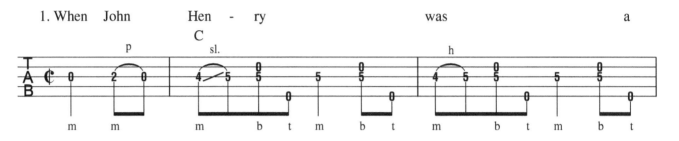

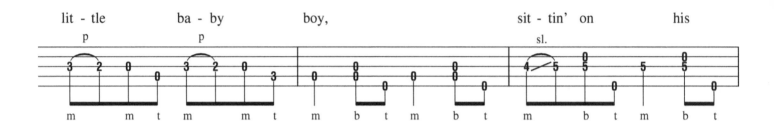

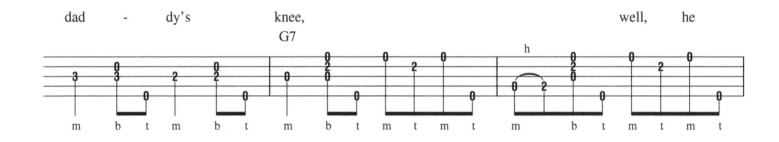

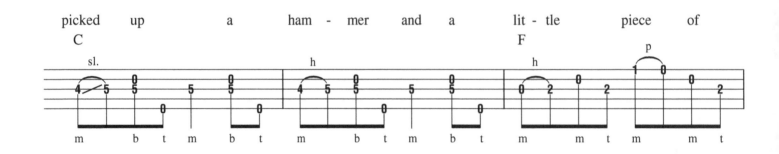

steel,   said,   "That   ham - mer's   gon - na   be   the   death   of

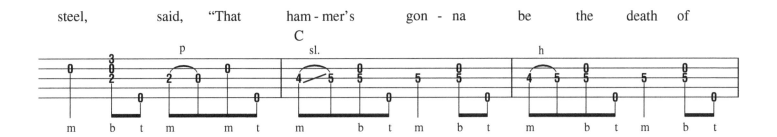

me,   Lord,   Lord.   Yeah,   that   ham - mer's   gon - na

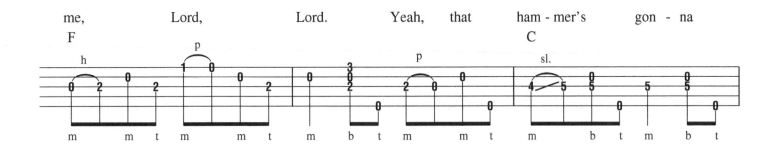

be   the   death   of   me."

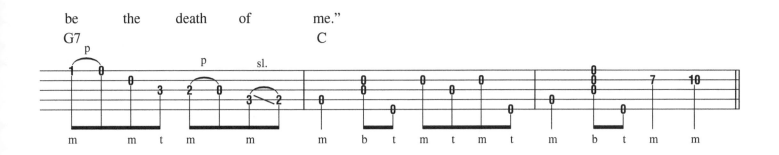

Banjo Break

C

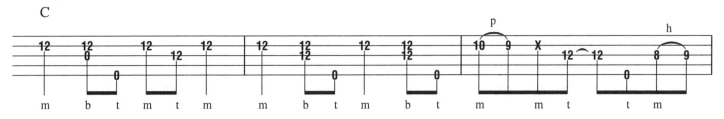

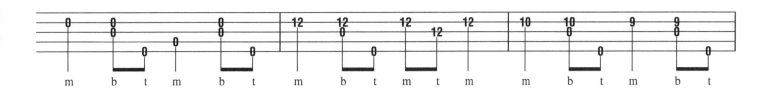

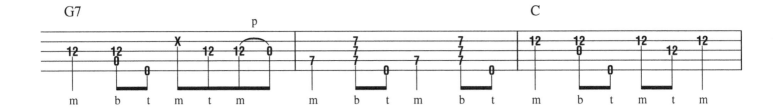

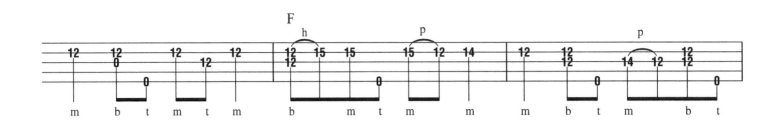

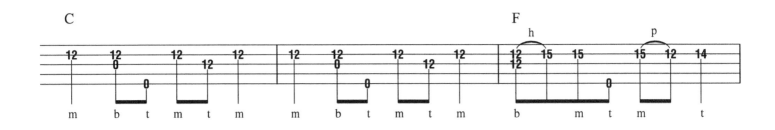

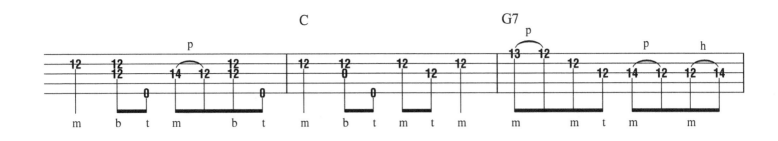

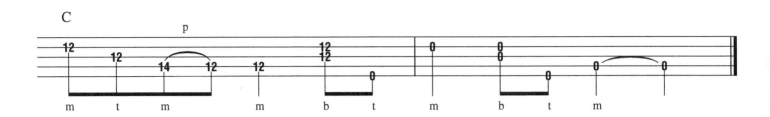

Nobody Knows the Trouble I've Seen

African-American Spiritual

Double C tuning:
(5th-1st) G-C-G-C-D

Key of C

Chorus
Moderately

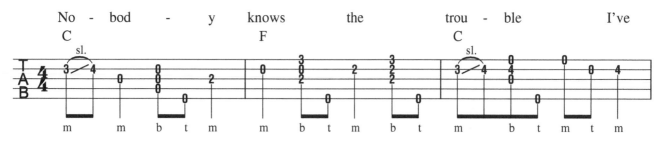

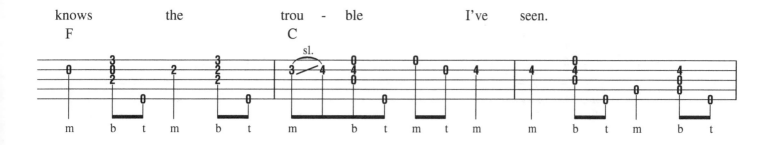

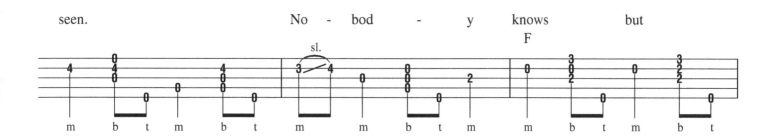

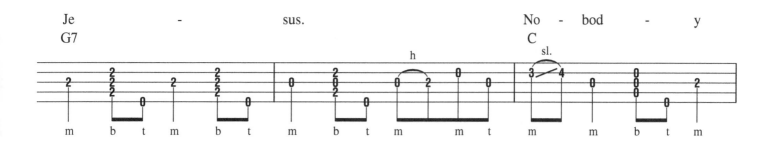

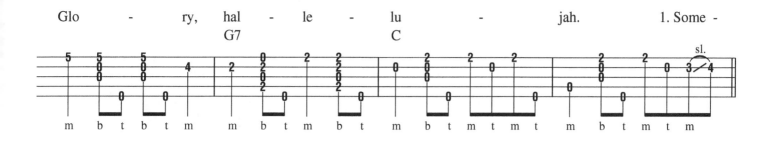

Verse

times   I'm   up,   some - times   I'm

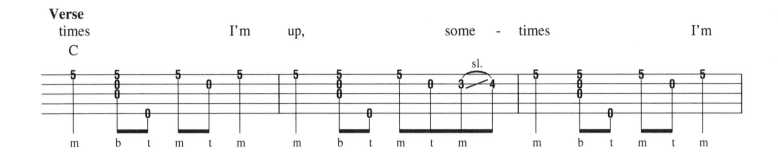

down.   Oh   yes,

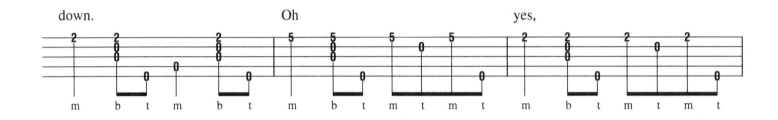

Lord.   Some - times   I'm

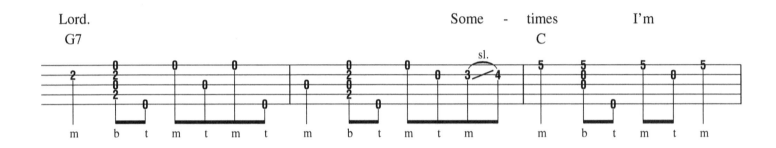

al -   most   to   the   ground.

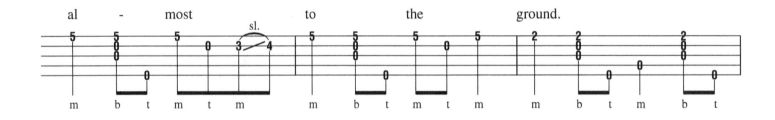

Oh   yes,   Lord.

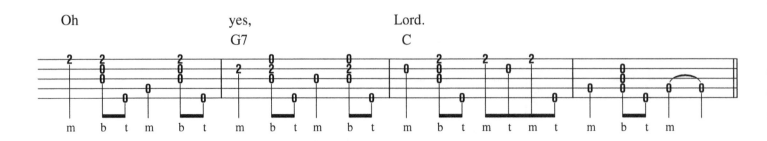

Banjo Break

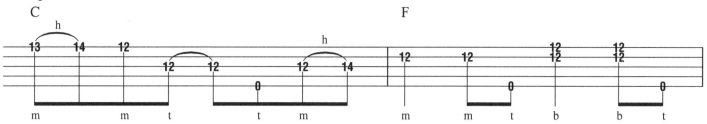

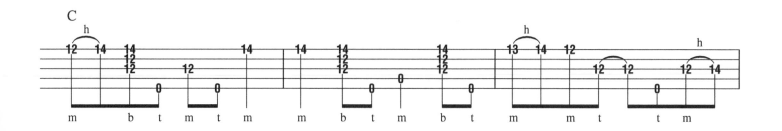

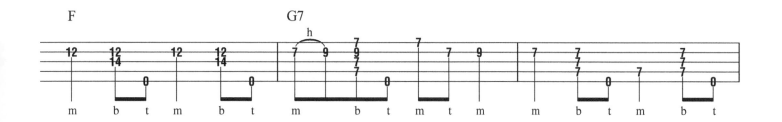

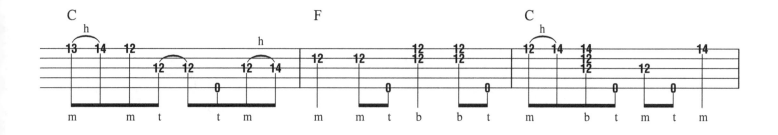

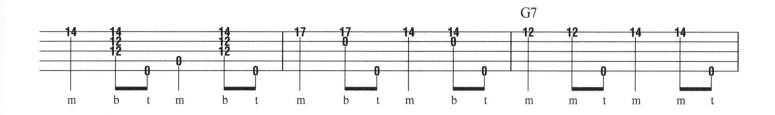

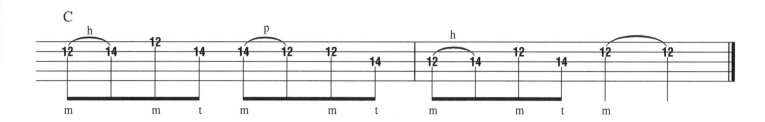

Kumbaya

Congo Folksong

C tuning:
(5th-1st) G-C-G-C-E

Key of C

Verse
  Moderately

1. Kum - ba - ya,   my Lord,   Kum - ba -

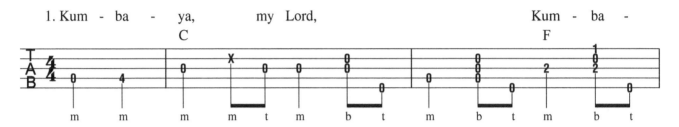

ya.   Kum - ba - ya,   my Lord,

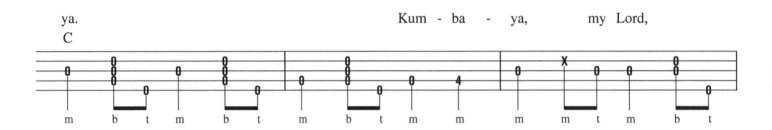

Kum - ba - ya.   Kum - ba -

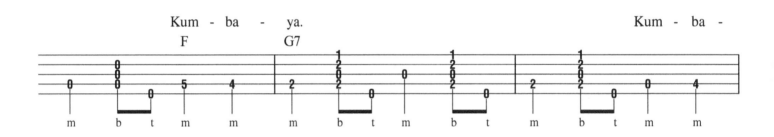

ya,   my Lord,   Kum - ba - ya.

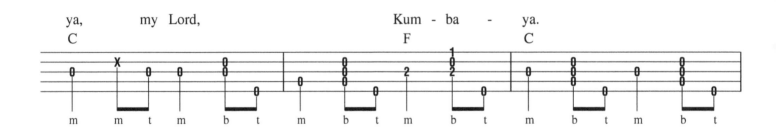

Oh   Lord,   Kum - ba -

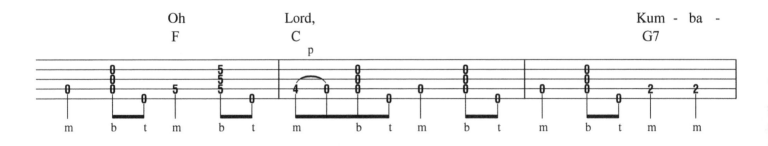

ya.

Banjo Break

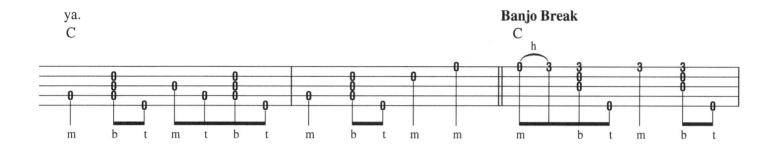

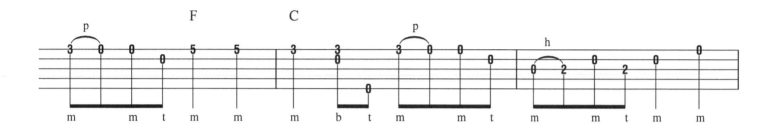

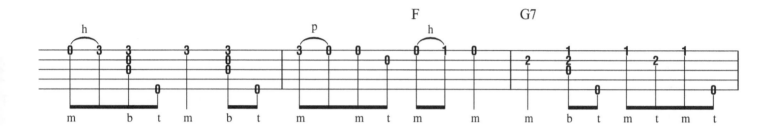

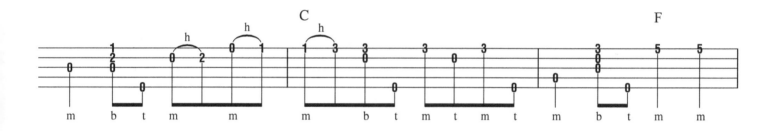

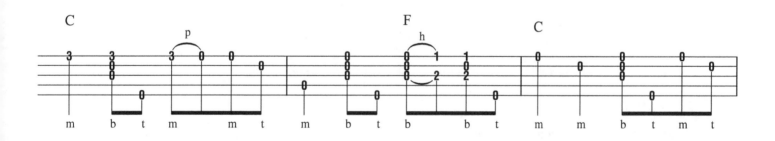

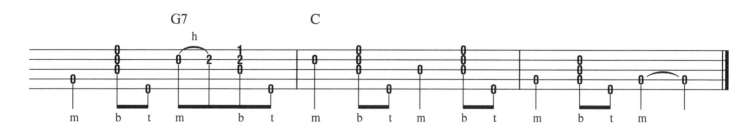

Little Brown Jug

Words and Music by Joseph E. Winner

G tuning:
(5th-1st) G-D-G-B-D

Key of G

Verse
Moderately fast

1. My wife and I lived all a-lone in a lit-tle log hut we

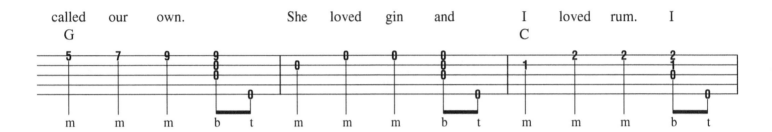

called our own. She loved gin and I loved rum. I

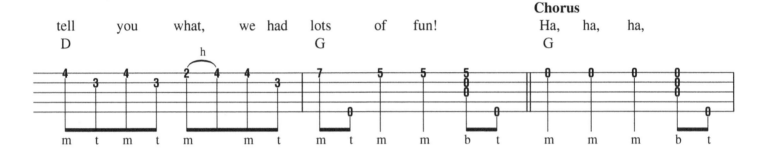

tell you what, we had lots of fun! **Chorus** Ha, ha, ha,

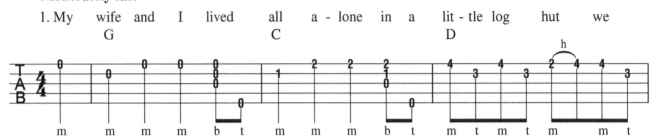

you and me, lit-tle brown jug, don't I love thee!

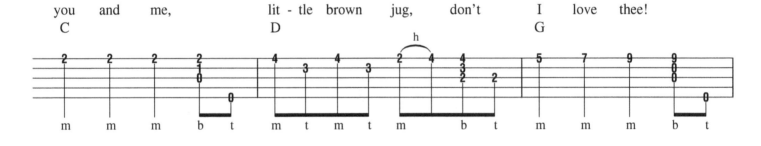

Ha, ha, ha, you and me, lit-tle brown jug, don't I love thee!

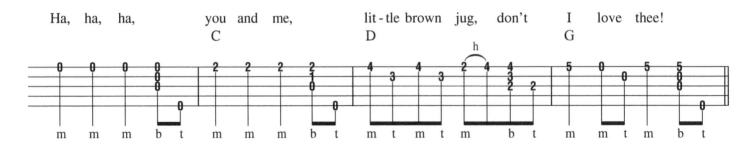

Banjo Break

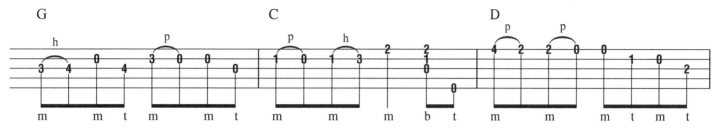

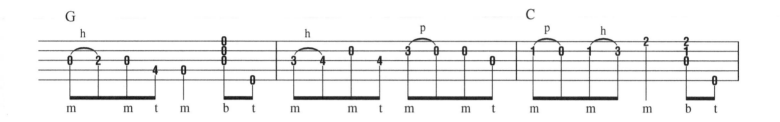

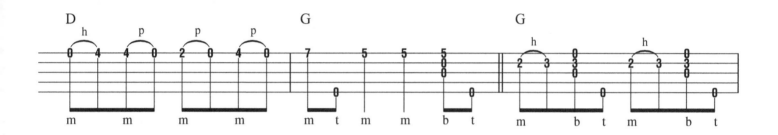

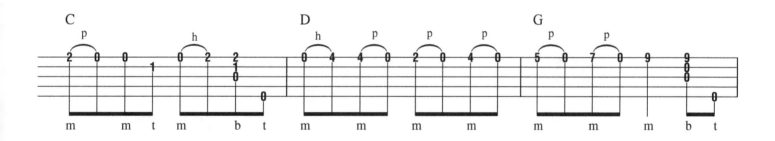

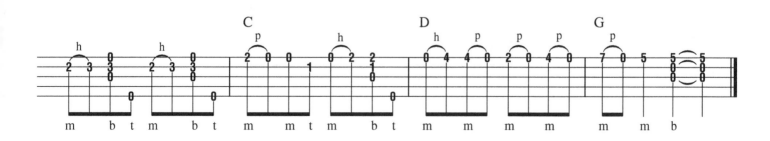

Man of Constant Sorrow

Traditional

G modal tuning:
(5th-1st) G-D-G-C-D

Key of G

Intro
    Moderately fast

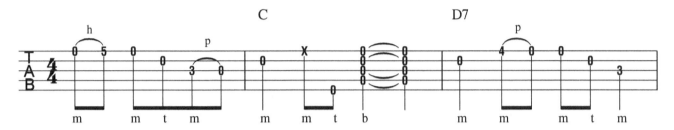

Verse
1. I

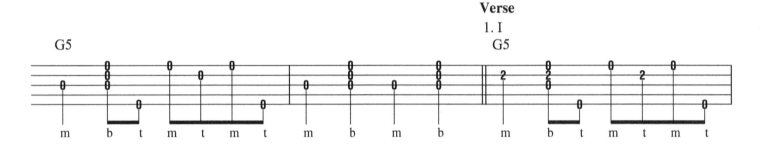

am   a   man   of con - stant

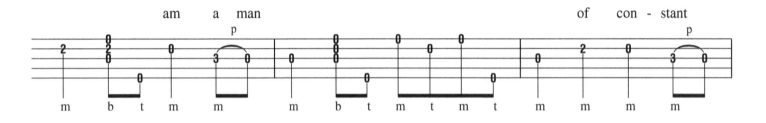

sor - row.   I've seen trou -

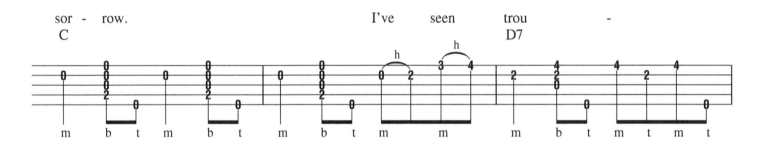

ble all my days.   I

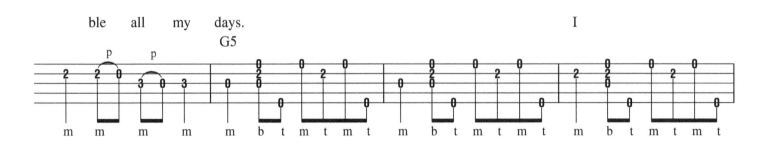

bid fare - well   to   old   Ken -

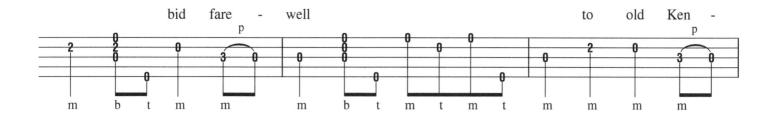

tuck - y,   the   place   where   I
C   D7

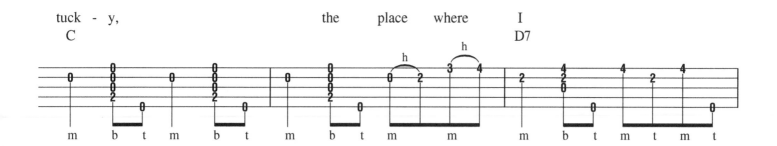

was   born   and   raised.
G5

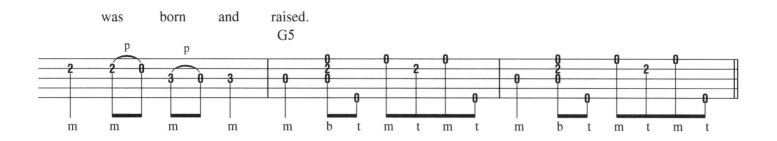

Banjo Break

G5

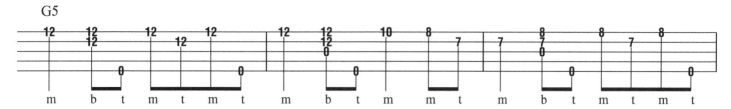

C

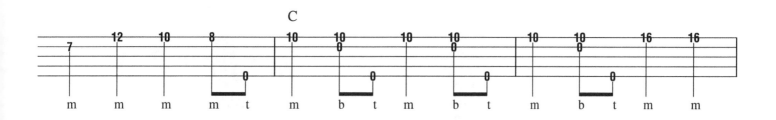

D7   G5

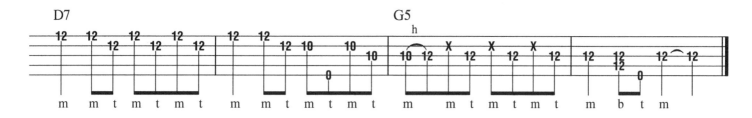

Michael Row the Boat Ashore

Traditional Folksong

G tuning:
(5th-1st) G-D-G-B-D

Key of G

Verse
Moderately

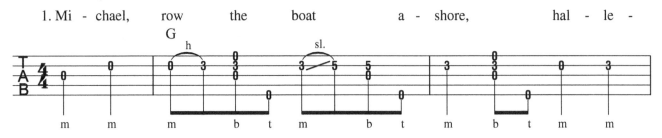

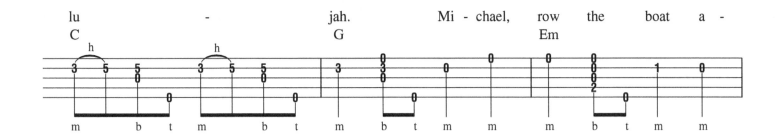

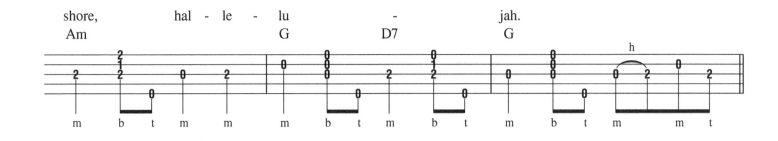

Banjo Break

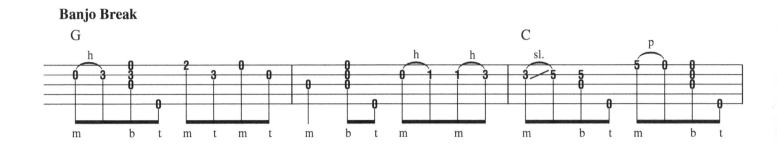

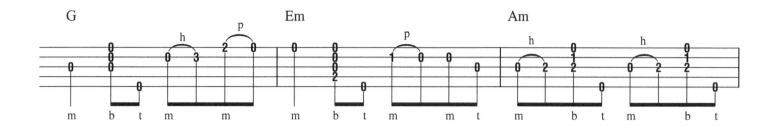

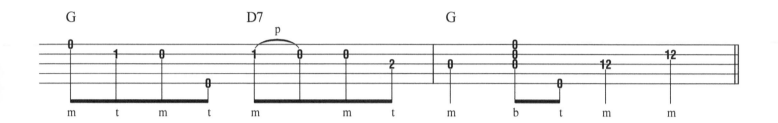

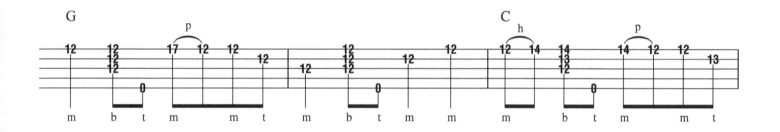

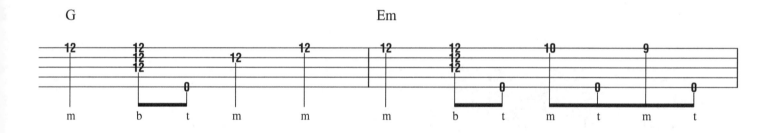

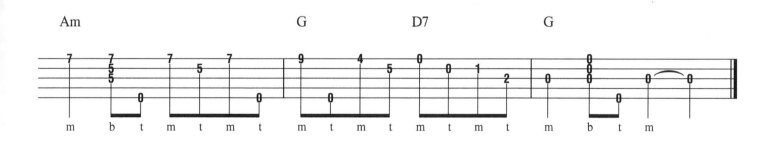

Midnight Special

Railroad Song

G tuning:
(5th-1st) G-D-G-B-D

Key of G

Verse
Moderately fast

1. Well, you wake up in the morn - ing, hear the ding dong

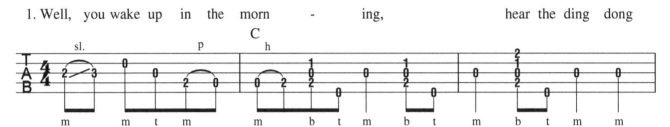

ring. You go march-in' to the ta - ble

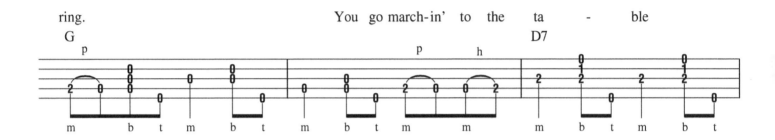

and you see the same darn thing. Well, it's all on the

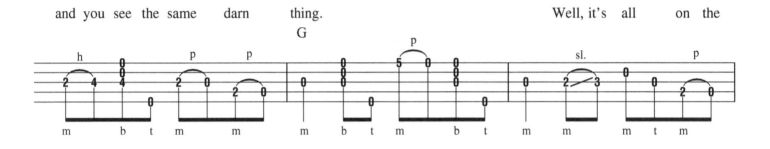

ta - ble, knife and fork and a pan.

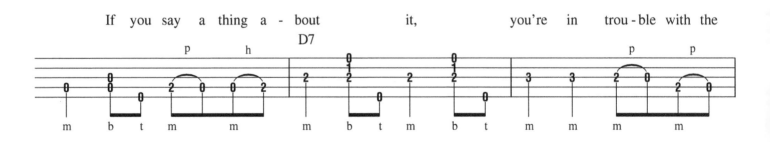

If you say a thing a - bout it, you're in trou - ble with the

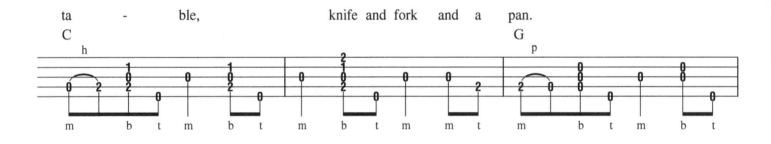

man.

Let the Mid - night Spe - cial

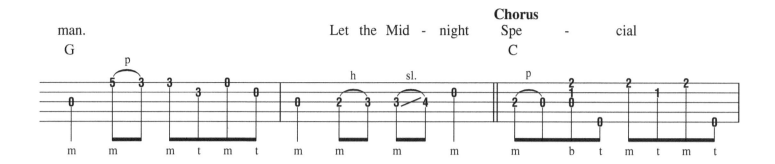

shine its light on me.

Let the Mid - night

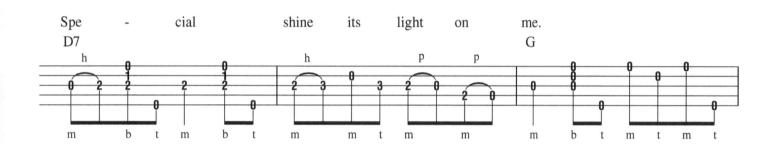

Spe - cial shine its light on me.

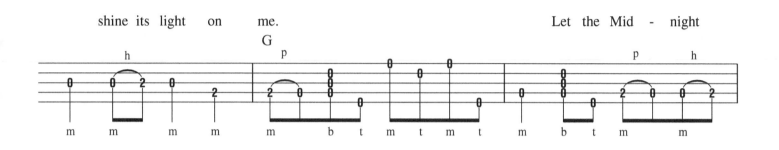

Let the Mid - night Spe - cial shine its light on

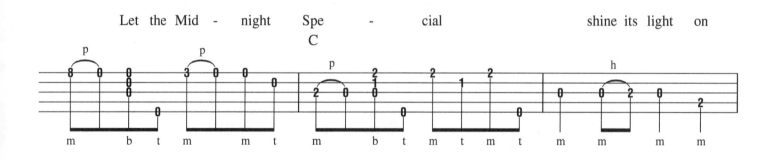

me.

Let the Mid - night spe - cial

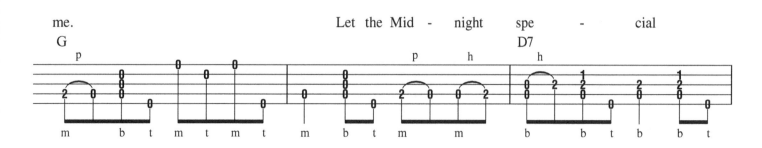

shine   its   light   on   me.

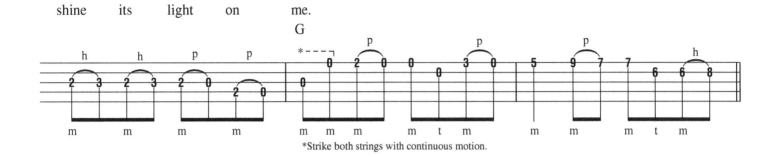

*Strike both strings with continuous motion.

Banjo Break

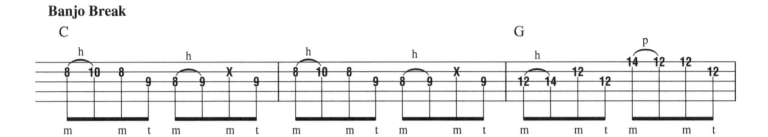

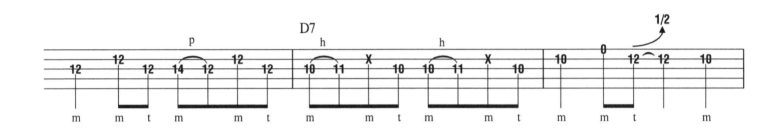

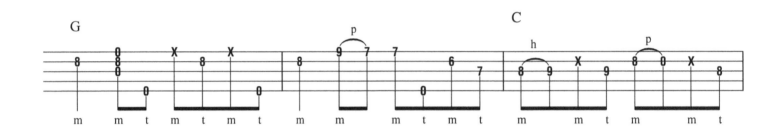

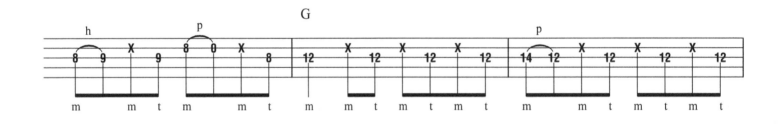

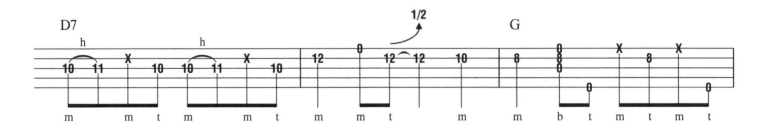

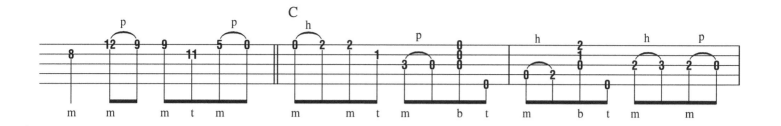

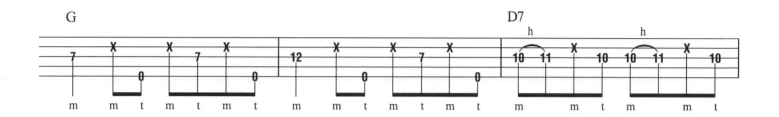

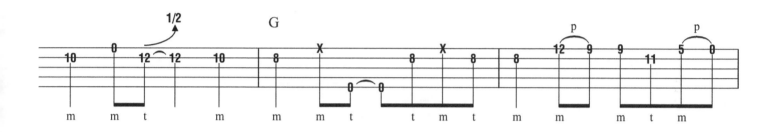

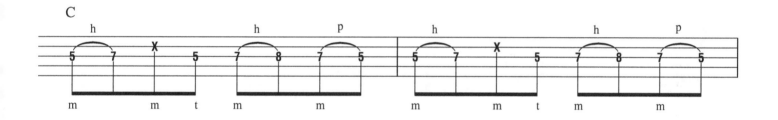

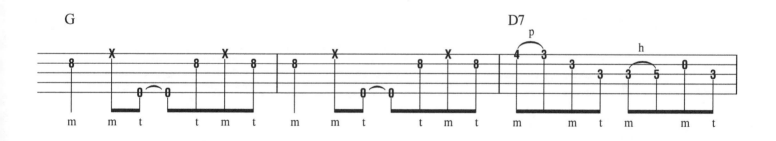

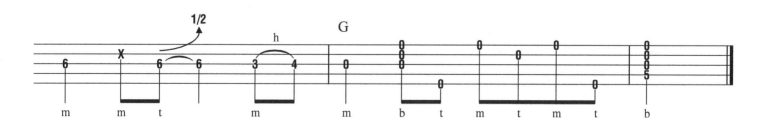

My Old Kentucky Home

Words and Music by Stephen C. Foster

Double C tuning:
(5th-1st) G-C-G-C-D

Key of C

Verse
Moderately

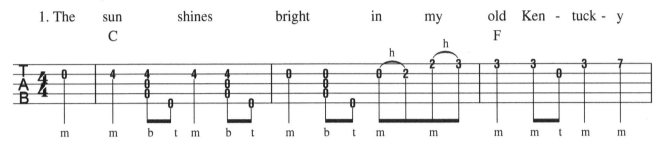

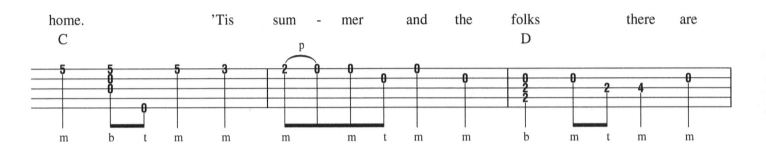

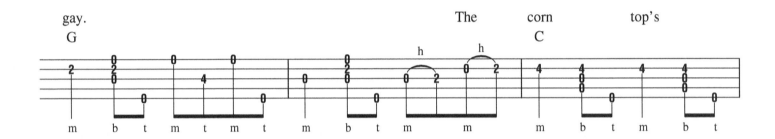

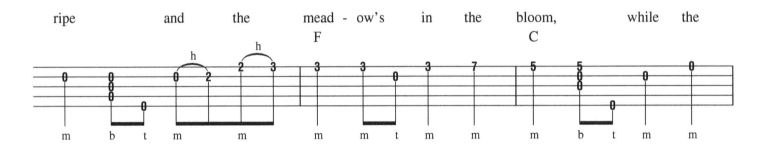

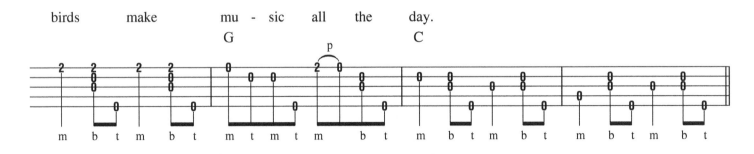

Chorus

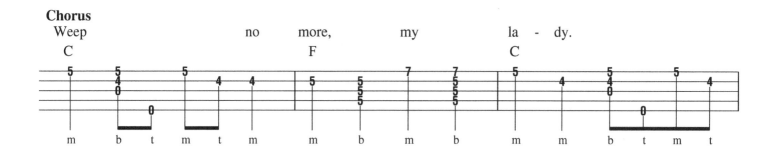

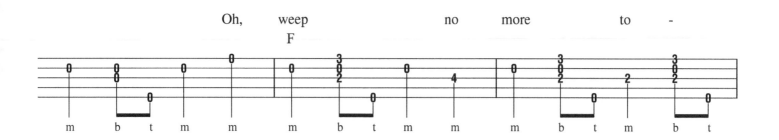

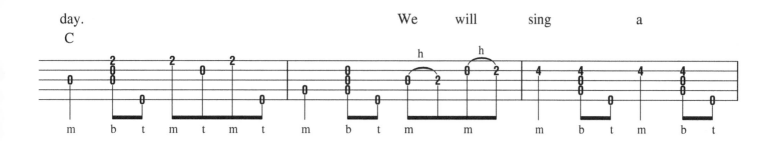

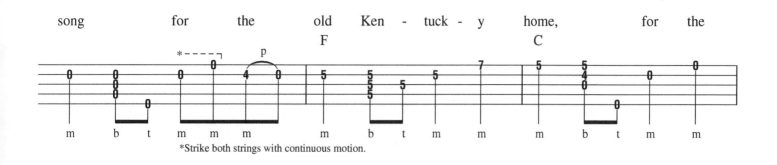

*Strike both strings with continuous motion.

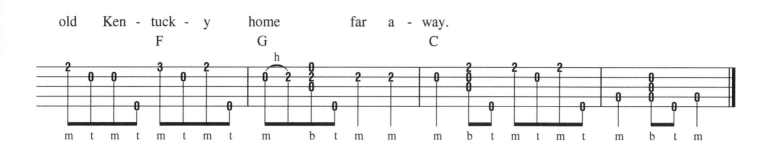

Oh! Susanna

Words and Music by Stephen C. Foster

C tuning:
(5th-1st) G-C-G-C-E

Key of C

Verse
Moderately fast

1. Oh, I come from Al - a - bam - a with a ban - jo on my

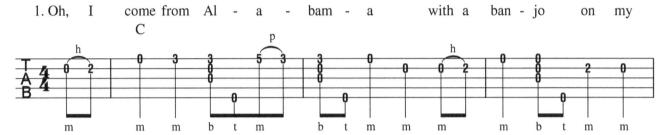

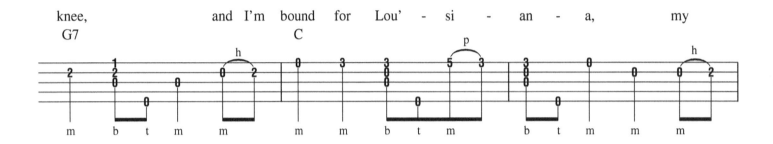

knee, and I'm bound for Lou' - si - an - a, my

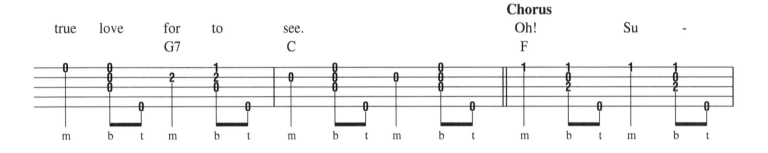

true love for to see. **Chorus** Oh! Su -

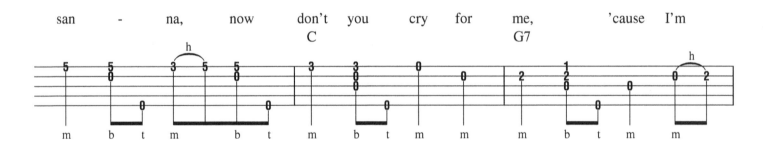

san - na, now don't you cry for me, 'cause I'm

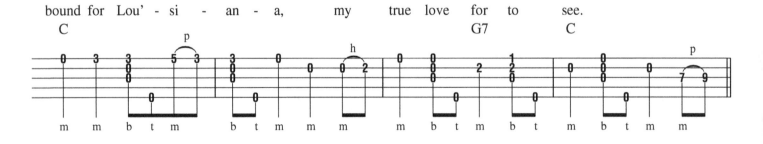

bound for Lou' - si - an - a, my true love for to see.

Banjo Break

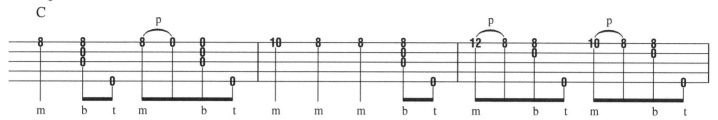

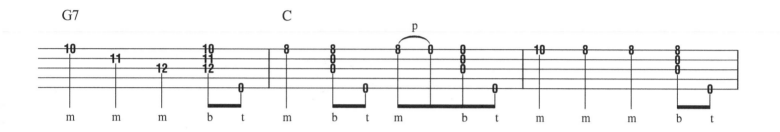

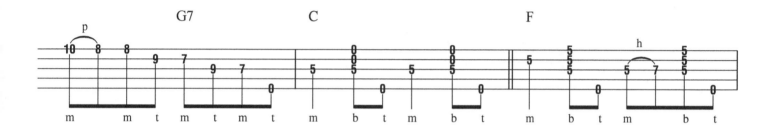

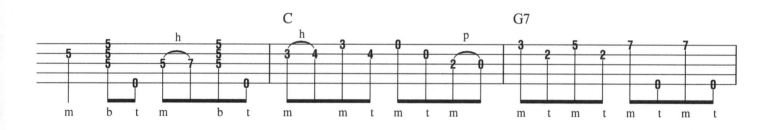

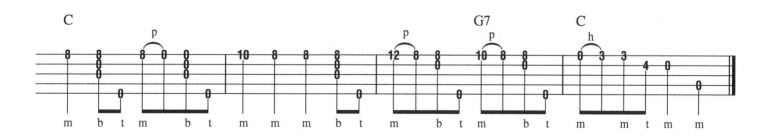

Old Folks at Home
(Swanee River)

Words and Music by Stephen C. Foster

Double C tuning:
(5th-1st) G-C-G-C-D

Key of C

Verse
Moderately fast

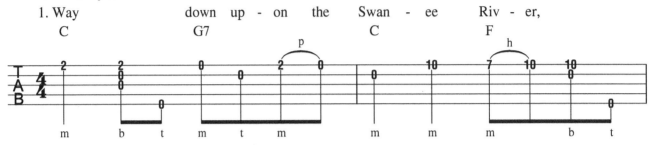

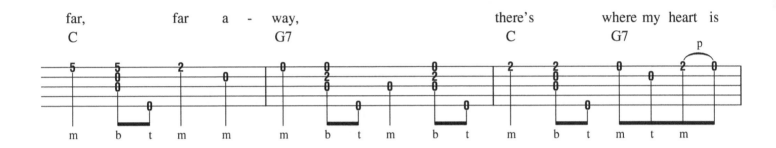

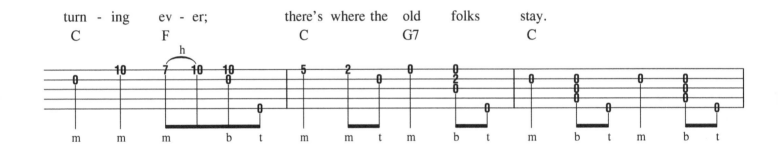

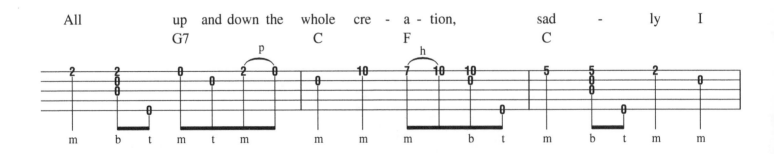

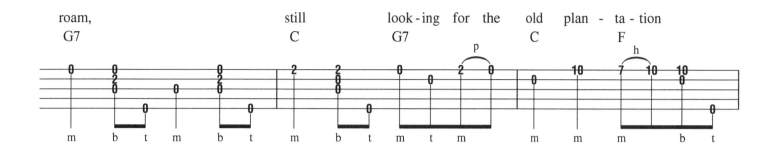

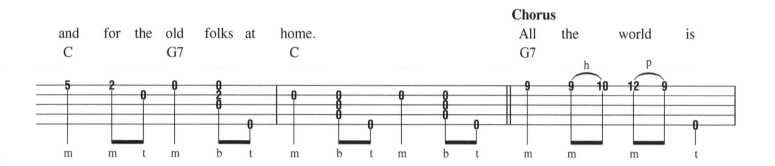

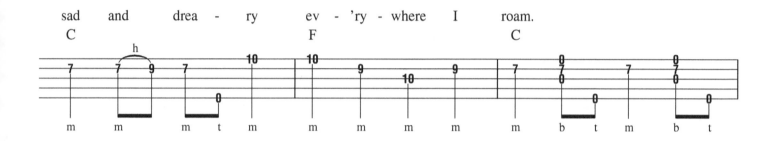

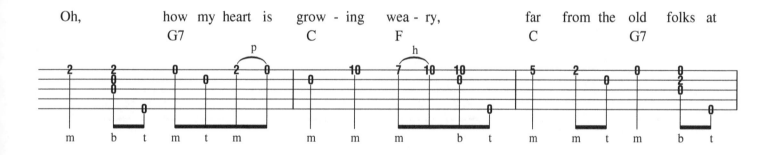

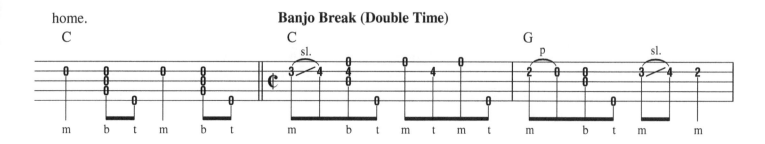

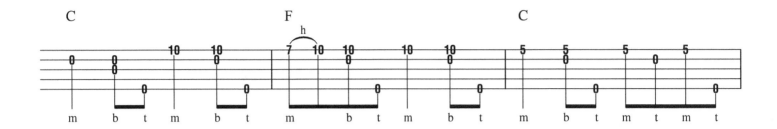

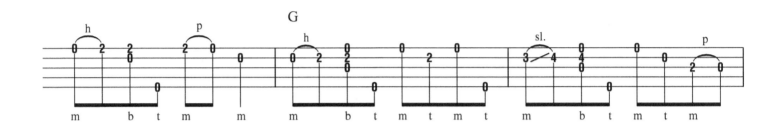

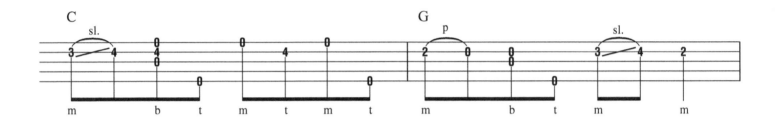

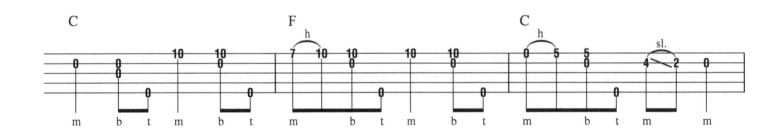

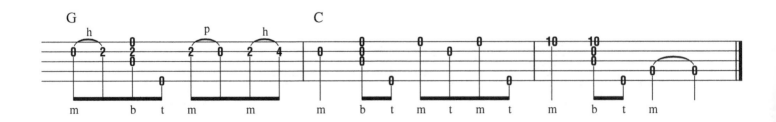

Turkey in the Straw

American Folksong

Double C tuning, capo II:
(5th-1st) G-C-G-C-D

Key of D

Very fast

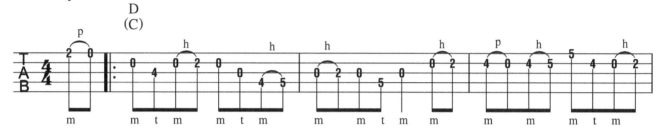

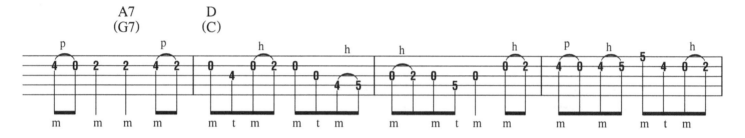

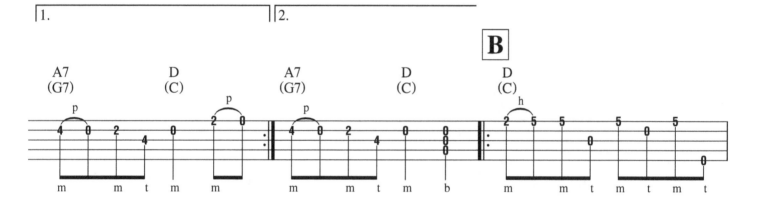

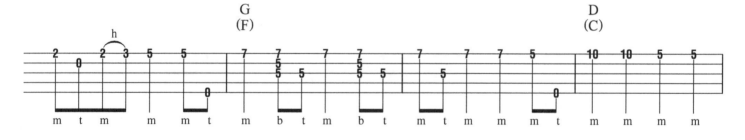

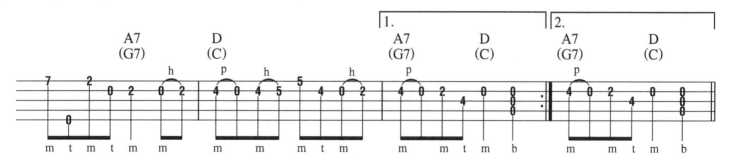

The Old Gray Mare

Words and Music by J. Warner

G tuning:
(5th-1st) G-D-G-B-D

Key of G

Verse
Moderately

1. Oh, the old gray mare, she ain't what she used to be,

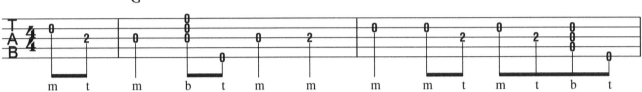

ain't what she used to be, ain't what she used to be. The old gray mare, she

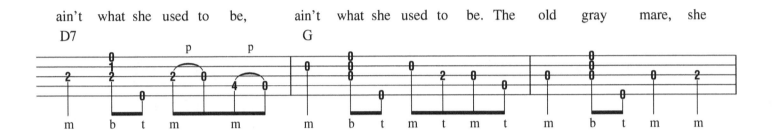

ain't what she used to be man-y long years a - go.

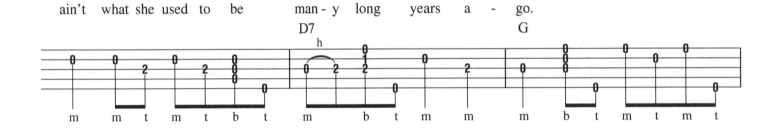

Many long years a - go, many long years a -

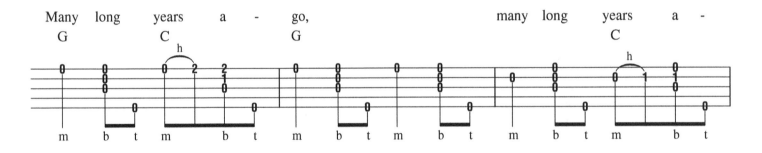

go. Oh, the old gray mare, she ain't what she used to be

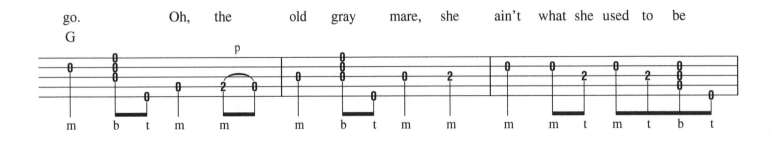

man - y long years a - go. **Banjo Break**

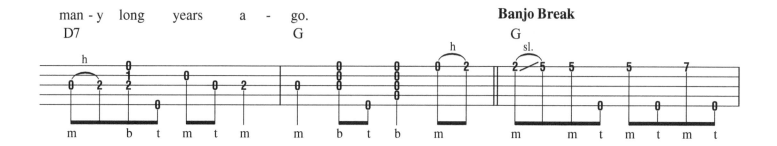

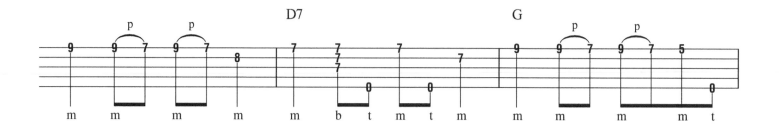

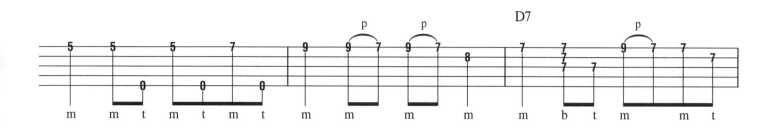

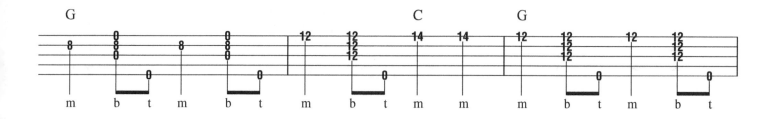

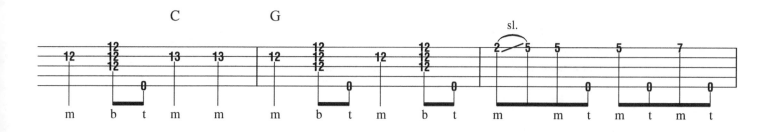

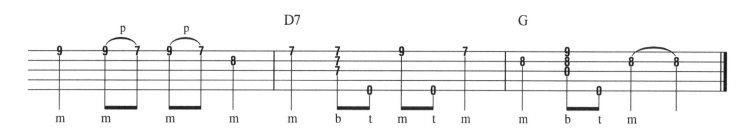

The Red River Valley

Traditional American Cowboy Song

G tuning:
(5th-1st) G-D-G-B-D

Key of G

Verse
Moderately

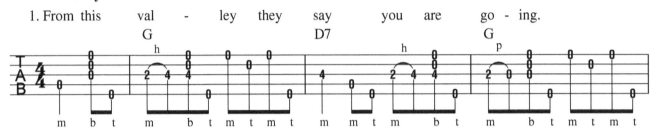

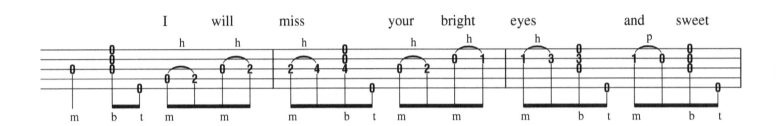

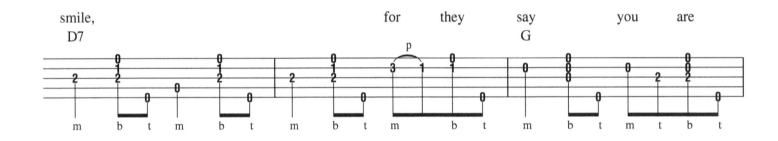

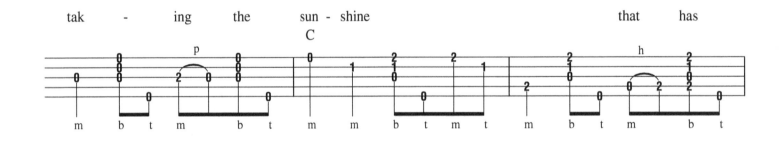

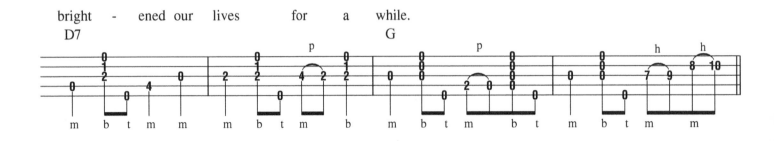

Banjo Break

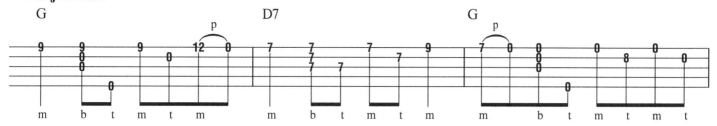

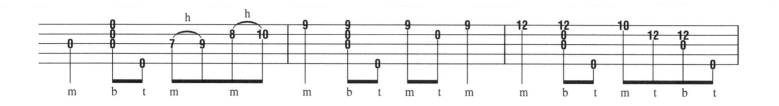

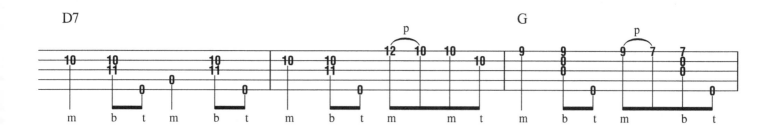

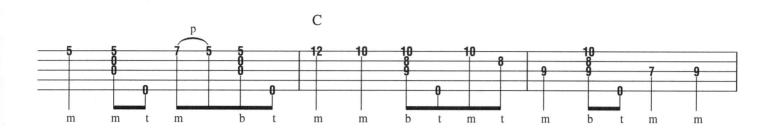

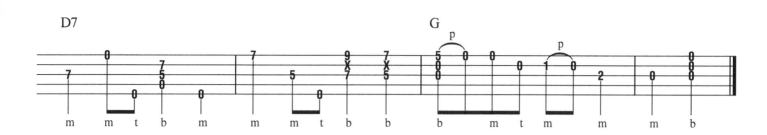

She'll Be Comin' 'Round the Mountain

Traditional

C tuning:
(5th-1st) G-C-G-C-E

Key of C

Verse
Fast

1. She'll be com - in' 'round the moun - tain when she comes.

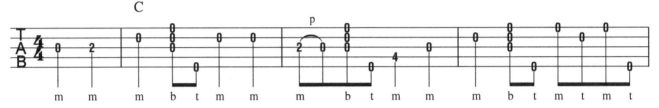

She'll be com - in' 'round the moun - tain when she

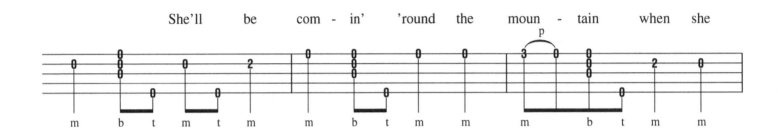

comes. She'll be com - in' 'round the

moun - tain, she'll be com - in' 'round the moun - tain, she'll be

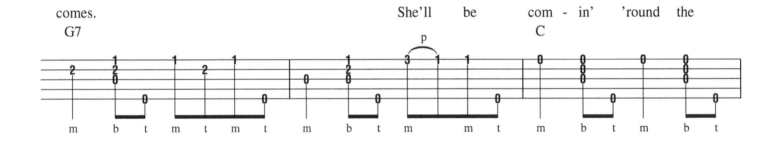

com - in' 'round the moun - tain when she comes.

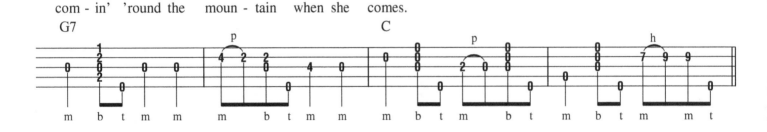

Banjo Break

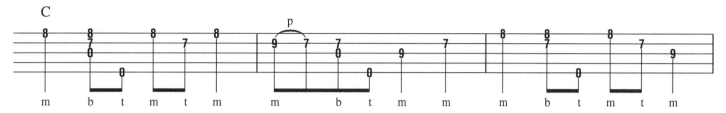

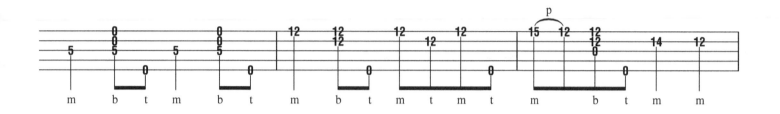

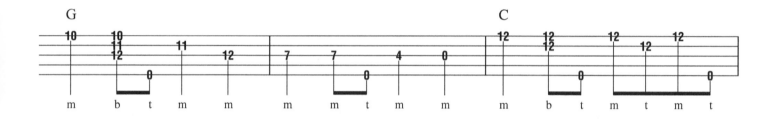

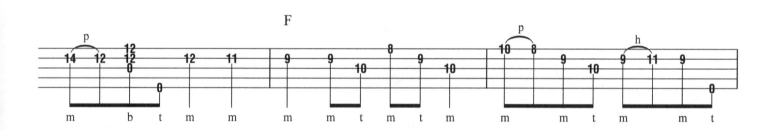

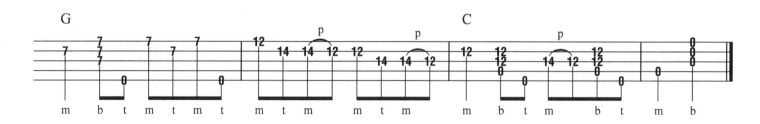

When Johnny Comes Marching Home

Words and Music by Patrick Sarsfield Gilmore

G modal tuning:
(5th-1st) G-D-G-C-D

Key of Gm

Verse
Moderately

1. When John - ny comes march - ing home a - gain, hur -

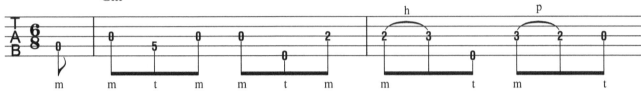

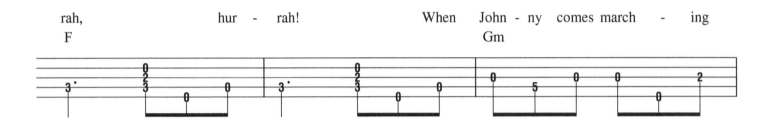

rah, hur - rah! When John - ny comes march - ing

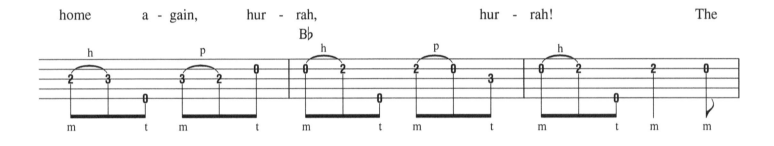

home a - gain, hur - rah, hur - rah! The

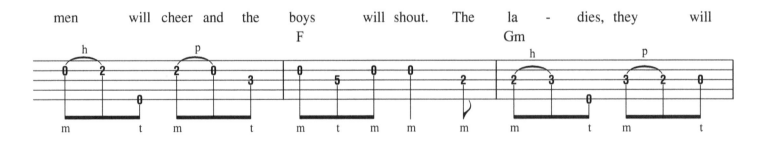

men will cheer and the boys will shout. The la - dies, they will

all come out, and we'll all be glad when

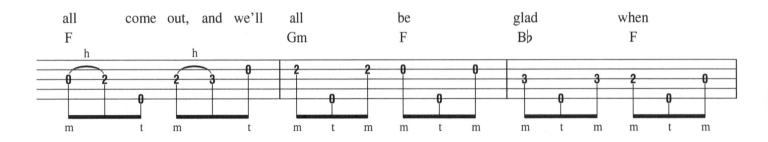

John - ny comes march - ing home.

Banjo Break

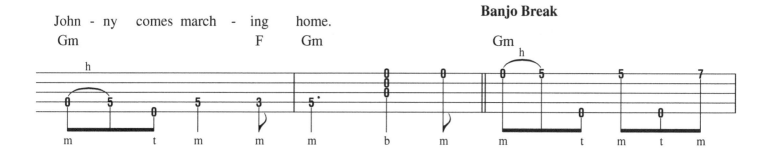

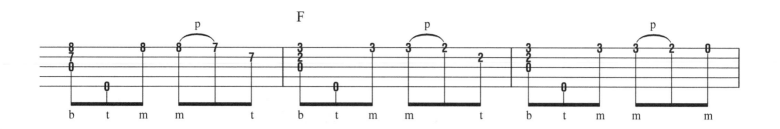

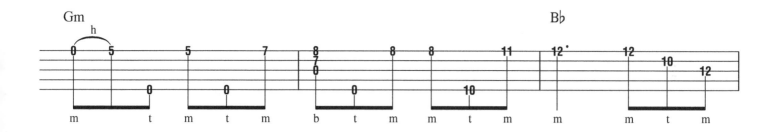

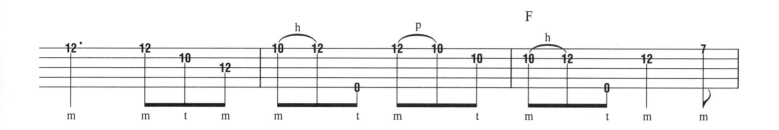

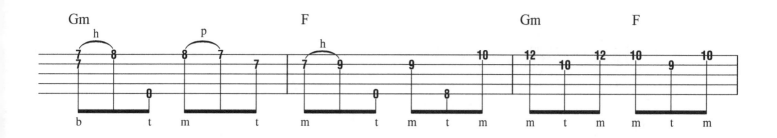

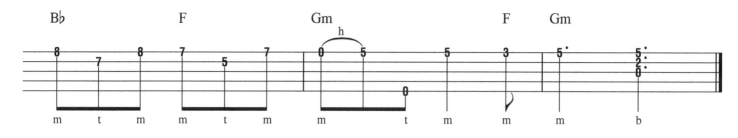

When the Saints Go Marching In

Words by Katherine E. Purvis
Music by James M. Black

G tuning:
(5th-1st) G-D-G-B-D

Key of G

Verse
Fast

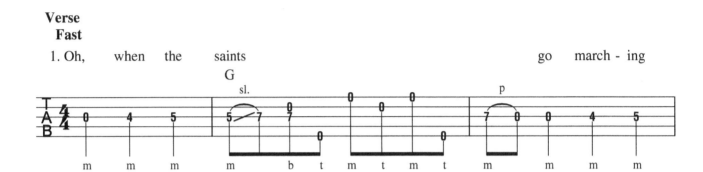

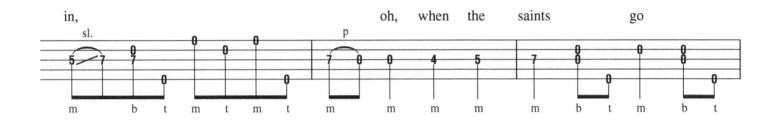

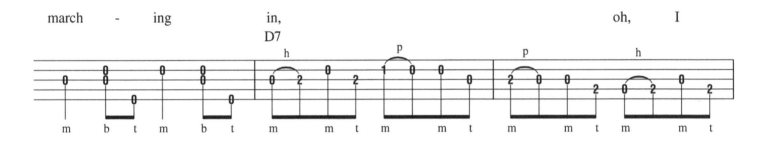

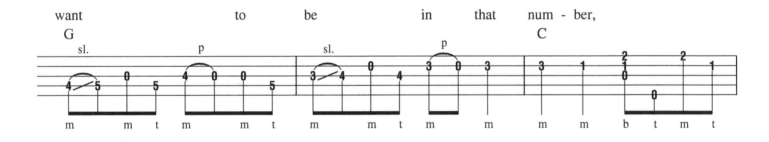

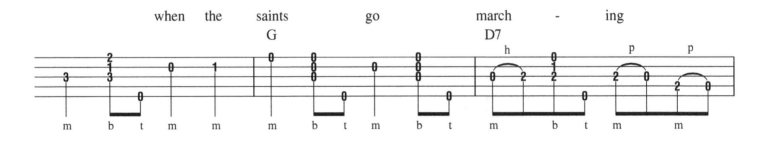

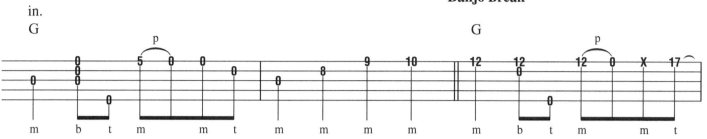

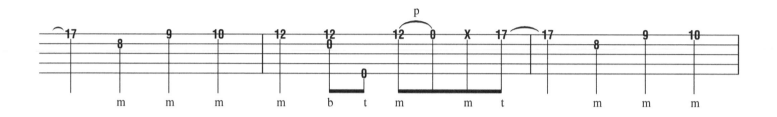

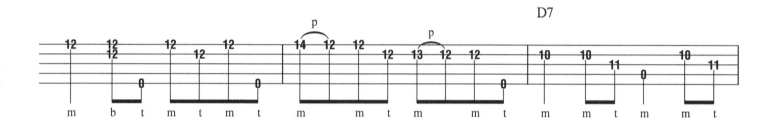

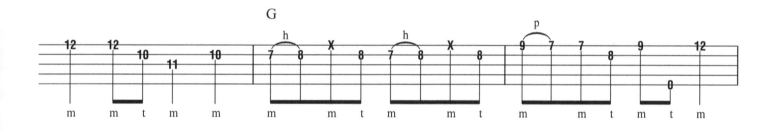

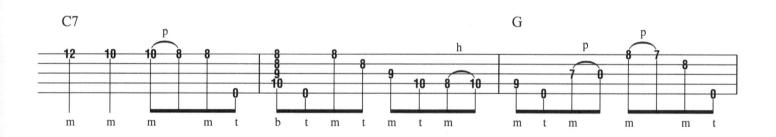

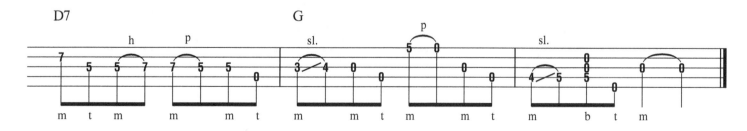

Worried Man Blues

Traditional

G tuning:
(5th-1st) G-D-G-B-D

Key of G

Verse
Moderately

1. It takes a wor - ried man to sing a wor - ried

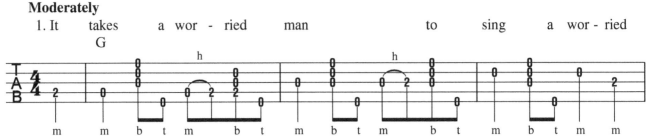

song. It takes a wor - ried man to

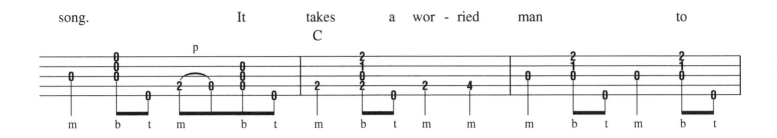

sing a wor - ried song. It takes a wor - ried

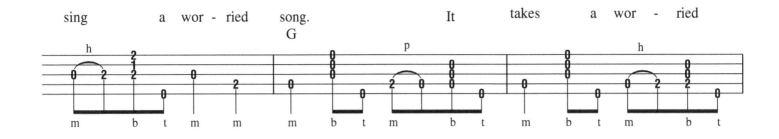

man to sing a wor - ried song. I'm wor - ried

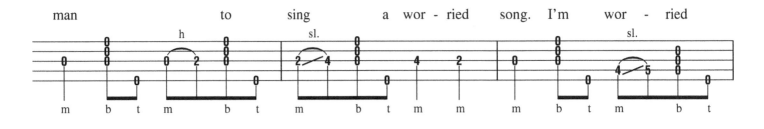

now, but I won't be wor - ried long.

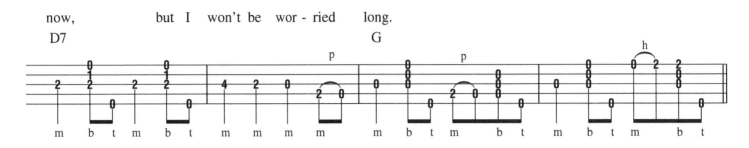

Banjo Break

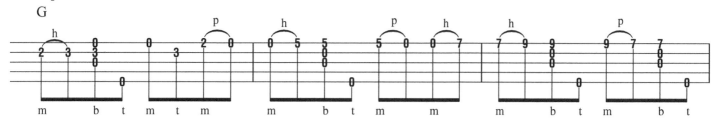

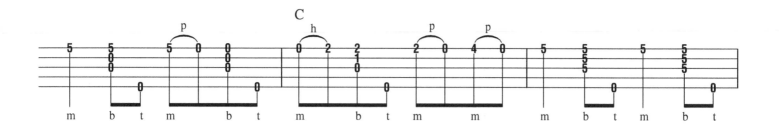

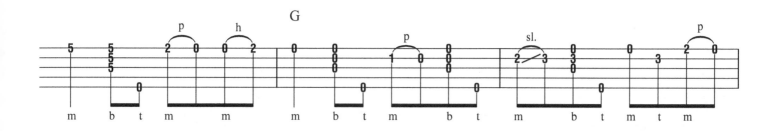

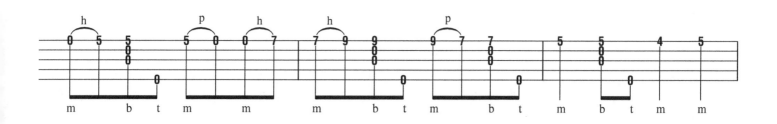

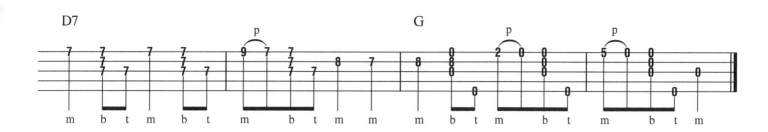

Yankee Doodle

Traditional

Double C tuning:
(5th-1st) G-C-G-C-D

Key of C

Verse
Fast

1. Yan - kee Doo - dle went to town rid - ing on a

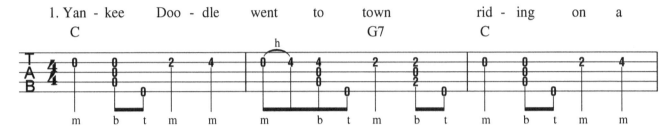

po - ny; stuck a feath - er in his cap and

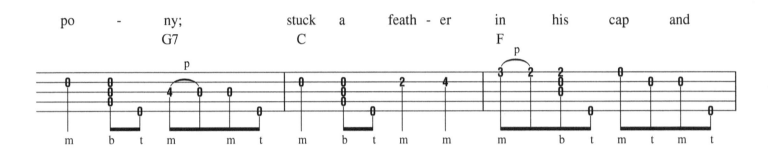

called it mac - a - ro - ni. **Chorus** Yan - kee Doo - dle

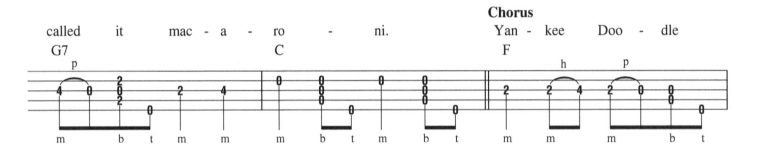

keep it up, Yan - kee Doo - dle dan - dy.

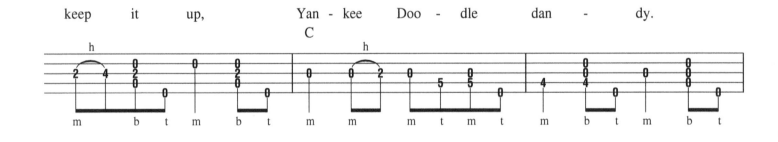

Mind the mu - sic and the step, and with the girls be hand - y.

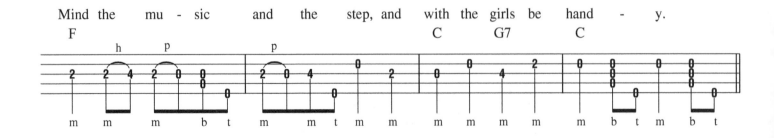

Banjo Break

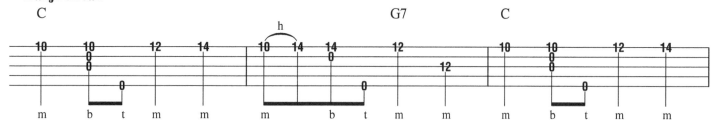

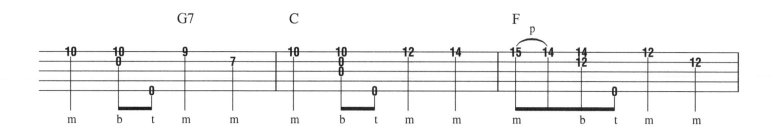

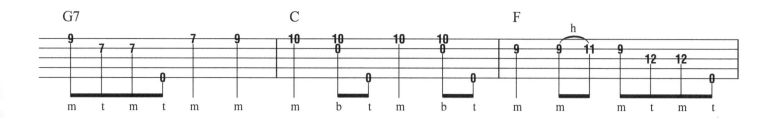

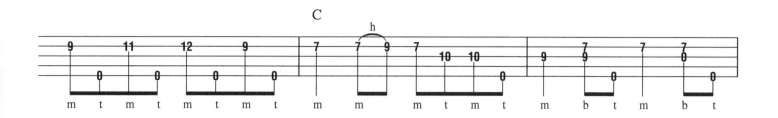

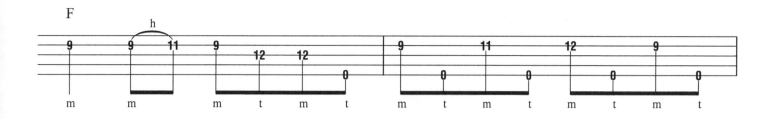

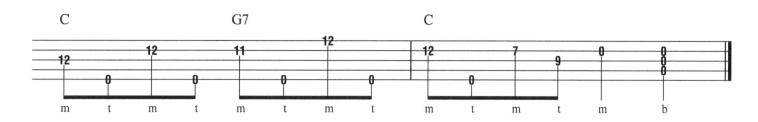

The Yellow Rose of Texas

Words and Music by J.K., 1858

G tuning:
(5th-1st) G-D-G-B-D

Key of G

Verse
Fast

1. There's a   yel - low   rose   of   Tex - as   that

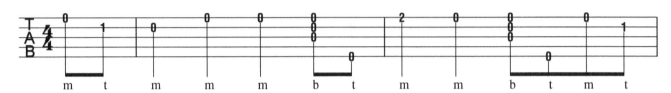

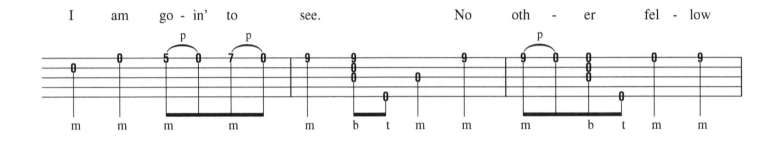

I   am   go - in' to   see.   No   oth - er   fel - low

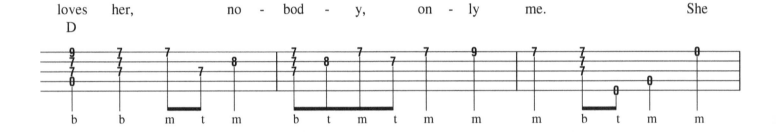

loves her,   no - bod - y,   on - ly   me.   She

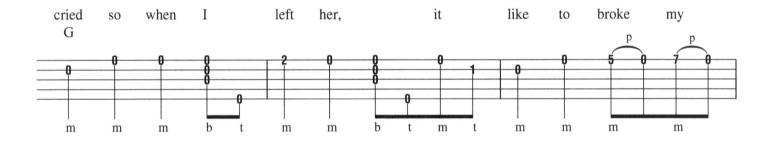

cried   so when   I   left her,   it   like to   broke   my

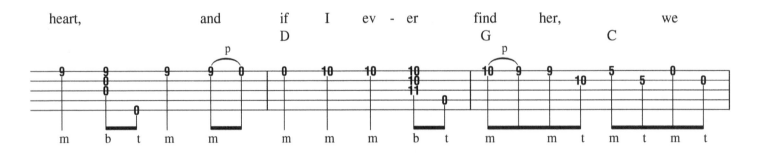

heart,   and   if   I   ev - er   find   her,   we

nev - er - more will part.

Banjo Break

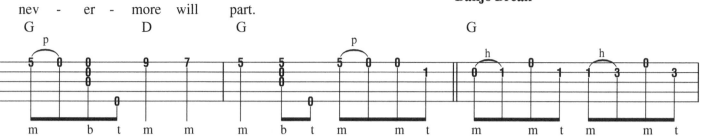

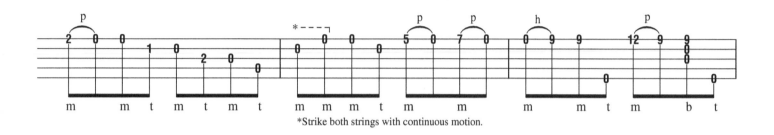

*Strike both strings with continuous motion.

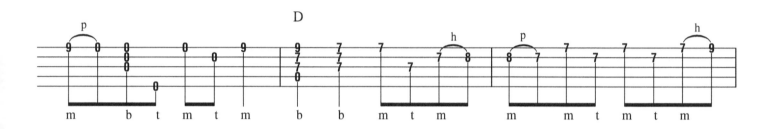

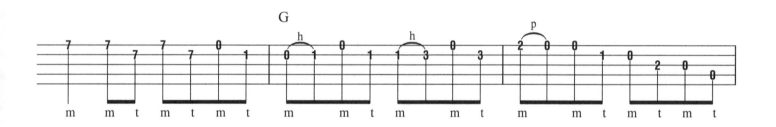

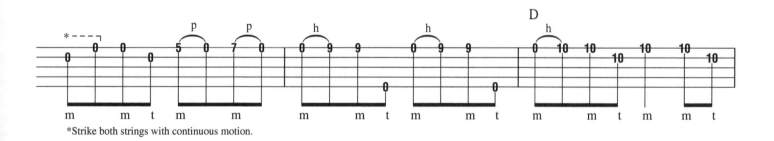

*Strike both strings with continuous motion.

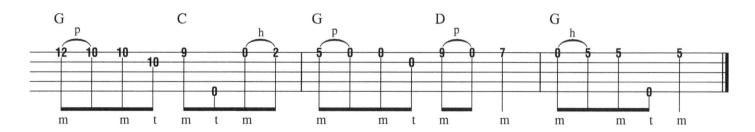

The Wabash Cannon Ball

Hobo Song

G tuning:
(5th-1st) G-D-G-B-D

Key of G

Verse
Fast

1. From the great At - lan - tic O - cean to the

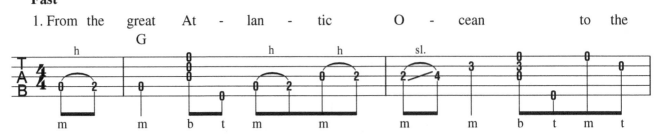

wide Pa - cif - ic shore, from the queen of flow - ing

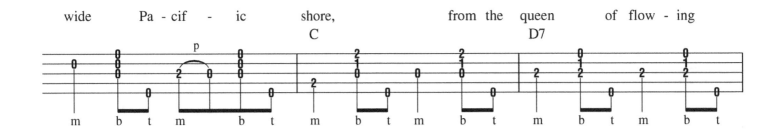

moun - tains to the south belt by the shore. She's

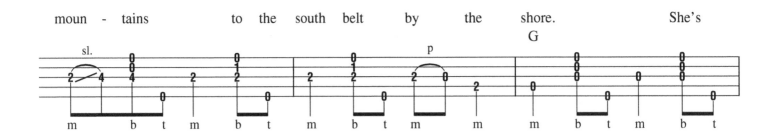

long, tall and hand - some; she's loved by one and

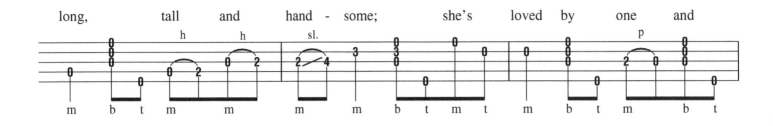

all. She's a mod - ern com - bi - na - tion called the

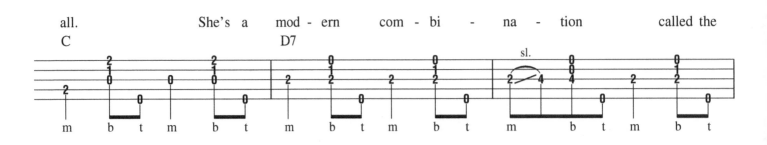

Wa - bash Can - non Ball. Lis - ten to the

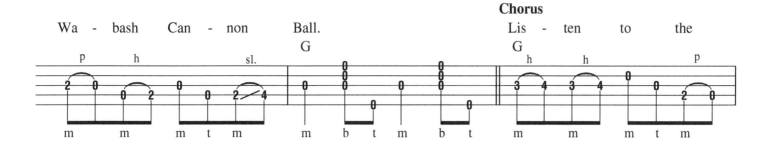

jin - gle, the rum - ble and the roar,

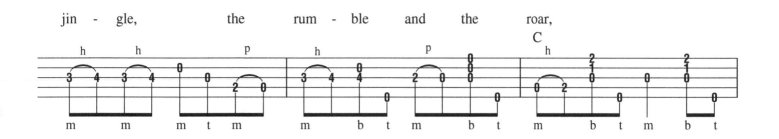

rid - ing through the wood - lands to the hills and by the

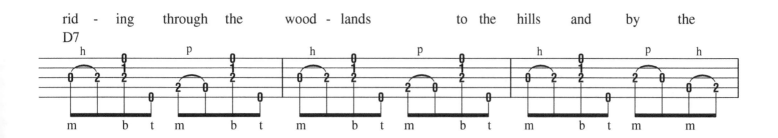

shore. Hear the might - y rush of en - gines, hear the

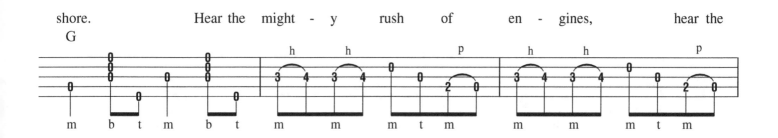

lone - some ho - bo squall, rid - ing through the

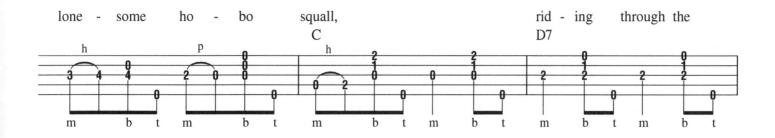

jun - gles on the Wa - bash Can - non Ball.

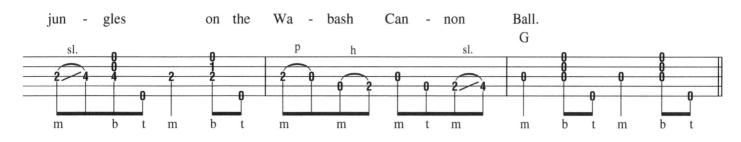

Banjo Break

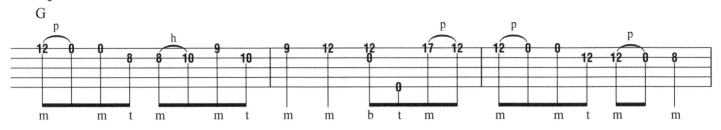

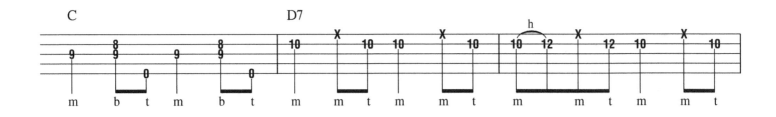

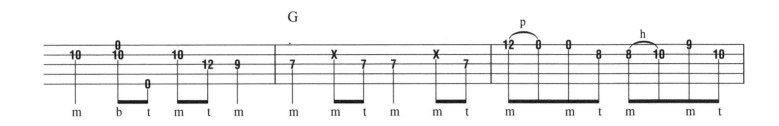

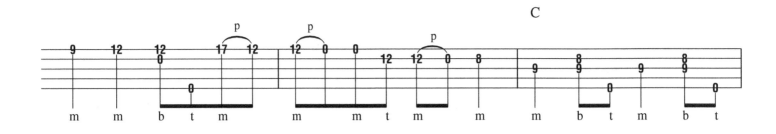

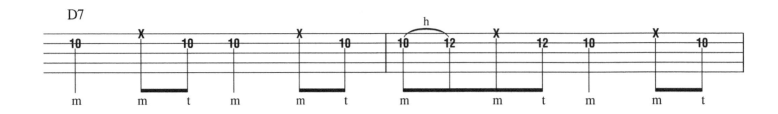

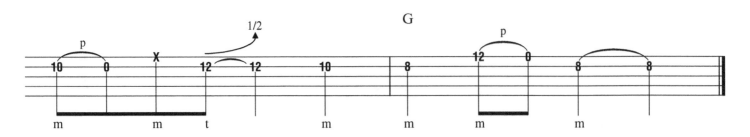

BANJO NOTATION LEGEND

TABLATURE graphically represents the banjo fingerboard. Each horizontal line represents a string, and each number represents a fret.

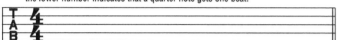

4th string, 2nd fret

1st & 2nd strings open, played together

TIME SIGNATURE:
The upper number indicates the number of beats per measure, the lower number indicates that a quarter note gets one beat.

CUT TIME:
Each note's time value should be cut in half. As a result, the music will be played twice as fast as it is written.

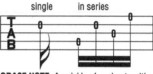

QUARTER NOTE:
time value = 1 beat

EIGHTH NOTES:
time value = 1/2 beat each

single   in series

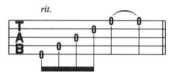

SIXTEENTH NOTES:
time value = 1/4 beat each

single   in series

DOTTED QUARTER NOTE:
time value = 1 1/2 beat

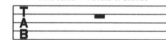

TIE: Pick the 1st note only, then let it sustain for the combined time value.

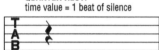

TRIPLET: Three notes played in the same time normally occupied by two notes of the same time value.

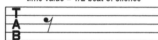

GRACE NOTE: A quickly played note with no time value of its own. The grace note and the note following it only occupy the time value of the second note.

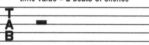

RITARD: A gradual slowing of the tempo or speed of the song.

rit.

QUARTER REST:
time value = 1 beat of silence

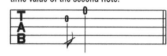

EIGHTH REST:
time value = 1/2 beat of silence

HALF REST:
time value = 2 beats of silence

WHOLE REST:
time value = 4 beats of silence

ENDINGS: When a repeated section has a first and second ending, play the first ending only the first time and play the second ending only the second time.

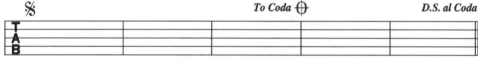

REPEAT SIGNS: Play the music between the repeat signs two times.

D.S. AL CODA:
Play through the music until you complete the measure labeled *"D.S. al Coda,"* then go back to the sign (𝄋).
Then play until you complete the measure labeled *"To Coda ⊕,"* then skip to the section labeled "⊕ Coda."

𝄋   *To Coda* ⊕   *D.S. al Coda*   ⊕ *Coda*

HAMMER-ON: Strike the first (lower) note with one finger, then sound the higher note (on the same string) with another finger by fretting it without picking.

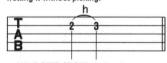

PULL-OFF: Place both fingers on the notes to be sounded. Strike the first note and without picking, pull the finger off to sound the second (lower) note.

SLIDE UP: Strike the first note and then slide the same fret-hand finger up to the second note. The second note is not struck.

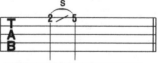

SLIDE DOWN: Strike the first note and then slide the same fret-hand finger down to the second note. The second note is not struck.

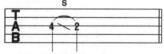

HALF-STEP CHOKE: Strike the note and bend the string up 1/2 step.

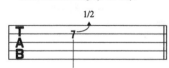

WHOLE-STEP CHOKE: Strike the note and bend the string up one step.

NATURAL HARMONIC: Strike the note while the fret-hand lightly touches the string directly over the fret indicated.

Harm.

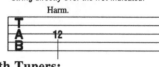

BRUSH: Play the notes of the chord indicated by quickly rolling them from bottom to top.

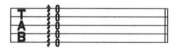

Scruggs/Keith Tuners:

HALF-TWIST UP: Strike the note, twist tuner up 1/2 step, and continue playing.

HALF-TWIST DOWN: Strike the note, twist tuner down 1/2 step, and continue playing.

WHOLE-TWIST UP: Strike the note, twist tuner up one step, and continue playing.

WHOLE-TWIST DOWN: Strike the note, twist tuner down one step, and continue playing.

Right Hand Fingerings

t = thumb   i = index finger   m = middle finger

GREAT BANJO PUBLICATIONS

FROM HAL LEONARD

Hal Leonard Banjo Method
by Mac Robertson, Robbie Clement, Will Schmid
This innovative method teaches 5-string banjo bluegrass style using a carefully paced approach that keeps beginners playing great songs *while learning.* Book 1 covers easy chord strums, tablature, right-hand rolls, hammer-ons, slides and pull-offs, and more. Book 2 includes solos and licks, fiddle tunes, back-up, capo use, and more.

00699500	Book 1 Book Only	$9.99
00695101	Book 1 Book/Online Audio	$17.99
00699502	Book 2 Book Only	$9.99

Banjo Chord Finder
00695741	9 x 12	$8.99
00695742	6 x 9	$7.99

Banjo Scale Finder
00695783	6 x 9	$6.99

Banjo Aerobics
A 50-Week Workout Program for Developing, Improving and Maintaining Banjo Technique
by Michael Bremer
Take your banjo playing to the next level with this fantastic daily resource, providing a year's worth of practice material with a two-week vacation. The accompanying audio includes demo tracks for all the examples in the book to reinforce how the banjo should sound.
00113734 Book/Online Audio $22.99

Earl Scruggs and the 5-String Banjo
Earl Scruggs' legendary method has helped thousands of banjo players get their start. It features everything you need to know to start playing, even how to build your own banjo! Topics covered include: Scruggs tuners • how to read music • chords • how to read tablature • anatomy of Scruggs-style picking • exercises in picking • 44 songs • biographical notes • and more! The online audio features Earl Scruggs playing and explaining over 60 examples!

00695764	Book Only	$29.99
00695765	Book/Online Audio	$39.99

First 50 Songs You Should Play on Banjo
arr. Michael J. Miles & Greg Cahill
Easy-to-read banjo tab, chord symbols and lyrics for the most popular songs banjo players like to play. Explore clawhammer and three-finger-style banjo in a variety of tunings and capoings with this one-of-a-kind collection. Songs include: Angel from Montgomery • Carolina in My Mind • Cripple Creek • Danny Boy • The House of the Rising Sun • Mr. Tambourine Man • Take Me Home, Country Roads • This Land Is Your Land • Wildwood Flower • and many more.
00153311 ....$15.99

Fretboard Roadmaps
by Fred Sokolow
This handy book/with online audio will get you playing all over the banjo fretboard in any key! You'll learn to: increase your chord, scale and lick vocabulary • play chord-based licks, moveable major and blues scales, melodic scales and first-position major scales • and much more! The audio includes 51 demonstrations of the exercises.

00695358 Book/Online Audio $17.99

The Great American Banjo Songbook
70 Songs
arr. Alan Munde & Beth Mead-Sullivan
Explore the repertoire of the "Great American Songbook" with this 70-song collection, masterfully arranged by Alan Munde and Beth Mead-Sullivan for 3-finger, Scruggs-style 5-string banjo. Rhythm tab, right hand fingerings and chord diagrams are included for each of these beloved melodies. Songs include: Ain't She Sweet • Blue Skies • Cheek to Cheek • Home on the Range • Honeysuckle Rose • It Had to Be You • Little Rock Getaway • Over the Rainbow • Sweet Georgia Brown • and more.
00156862 ....$19.99

How to Play the 5-String Banjo
Third Edition
by Pete Seeger
This basic manual for banjo players includes melody line, lyrics and banjo accompaniment and solos notated in standard form and tablature. Chapters cover material such as: a basic strum, the fifth string, hammering on, pulling off, double thumbing, and much more.

14015486 ....$19.99

O Brother, Where Art Thou?
Banjo tab arrangements of 12 bluegrass/folk songs from this Grammy-winning album. Includes: The Big Rock Candy Mountain • Down to the River to Pray • I Am a Man of Constant Sorrow • I Am Weary (Let Me Rest) • I'll Fly Away • In the Jailhouse Now • Keep on the Sunny Side • You Are My Sunshine • and more, plus lyrics and a banjo notation legend.

00699528 Banjo Tablature $17.99

Clawhammer Cookbook
Tools, Techniques & Recipes for Playing Clawhammer Banjo
by Michael Bremer
The goal of this book isn't to tell you how to play tunes or how to play like anyone else. It's to teach you ways to approach, arrange, and personalize any tune – to develop your own unique style. To that end, we'll take in a healthy serving of old-time music and also expand the clawhammer palate to taste a few other musical styles. Includes audio track demos of all the songs and examples to aid in the learning process.
00118354 Book/Online Audio $22.99

The Ultimate Banjo Songbook
A great collection of banjo classics: Alabama Jubilee • Bye Bye Love • Duelin' Banjos • The Entertainer • Foggy Mountain Breakdown • Great Balls of Fire • Lady of Spain • Orange Blossom Special • (Ghost) Riders in the Sky • Rocky Top • San Antonio Rose • Tennessee Waltz • UFO-TOFU • You Are My Sunshine • and more.

00699565 Book/Online Audio $29.99

Visit Hal Leonard online at **www.halleonard.com**